Z9.99.

BLUE TIDE

THE SEARCH FOR SOMA

The Burning of Darkness, Nicholas Roerich, (1924, detail)

BLUE TIDE

The Search for Soma

Mike Jay

Autonomedia

Cover and frontispiece detail from Nicholas Roerich's
Burning of Darkness is reproduced by courtesy
of the Nicholas Roerich Museum, New York, New York.

Page Design: Robert Karimi

Autonomedia
POB Williamsburgh Station
Brooklyn, NY 11211-0568 USA

Fax: 718-963-2603
Email: info@autonomedia. org
Web: www.autonomedia.org

Printed in the Altered States of America

Contents

Acknowledgements

I'd like to thank the following people for their help, encouragement, patience and expertise:

On drugs, plants and antiquity: Anthony Henman, Richard Rudgley, Prof. Gordon Hillman, Alan Lupton, Leonard F. Reuter, Dan Quaintance, Mescalito Ted, Aref Abu-Rabia, Sylvia and Rick Doblin at MAPS, Barry Mason and Nicholas Saunders;

On Iranian and Zoroastrian scholarship: Hannah M. G. Shapero, Dr. Ali Jafarey, David Flattery, Prof. Martin Schwartz, Prof. Stanley Insler, Franz Grenet, Dr. Ilya Gershevitch and Boz Temple-Morris;

For the Ladakh trip: Tim Malyon, Henry Osmaston, Maria Phylactou, Amchi Tsewang Smanla, Sonam Tsetan, Major B. A. Shahane and Tsewang Dorji Lingtse.

I'd also like to record the following special thanks:

To Iko Iyama, Jimmy Chambers and the Church of Santo Daime;

To Juri Gabriel; Mr. David Entin of the Nicholas Roerich Museum; Robert Karimi, Chiaki Fukuda, Jim Fleming and Peter Lamborn Wilson of Autonomedia;

To Louise;

To my fellow-psychonauts — you know who you are;

And especially to Dr. Edward 'Skip' Featherstone and Dorothy Kamen-Kaye: two true *harmal* pioneers.

Disclaimer

This book includes several accounts of the ingestion of hallucinogenic plant drugs. Most of these are legal; they are also, as plainly stated, toxic and potentially fatal. Just because a substance is legal doesn't mean that it's safe. There's no law, after all, against drinking bleach.

The intention of this book is not to encourage similar experiments. Rather the opposite: I've attempted to describe the experiences clearly enough to make further experiments less necessary rather than more. However, if anyone feels the need to experiment, I have tried to include at various points in the book enough practical information to improve, but not guarantee, their chances of doing so safely.

Prologue
ELIXIR OF THE GODS

"We have drunk the Soma
We have become immortal
We have gone to the light
We have found the Gods..."
The Rig Veda

In the beginning, there was *soma*. The *Rig Veda* (*"praise of sacred knowledge"*) is among the very earliest books known to man, and yet by the time it was written down in Sanskrit it had already existed for hundreds, maybe thousands of years. It is the book of the ancient inhabitants of northern India, and the gods they brought with them from their unknown homeland somewhere to the West.

A huge collection of hymns, it tells us much about the people who were in the process of settling and spreading across the whole of Europe and the Middle East, from India to Iceland. Modern scholarship has pushed the surviving texts of

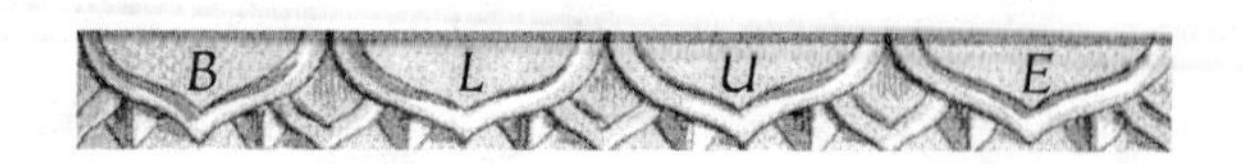

the *Rig Veda* forwards to around the fifth century AD, but is generally pushing back the date when the hymns were first sung, further and further into the mists of time — 1200, 2000, even 2500BC. It stands as the great surviving text of the lost civilisation before civilisation, the high Bronze Age of warriors and nomads, herdsmen and priests, jewels and precious metals, cattle-raiding and horse-sacrifice — and *soma*.

The gods of the Vedic people have multiple guises, multiple personalities, multiple levels of meaning, and Soma is many things. At root, it's a divine principle which occupies the centre of the cosmos in eternal conflict with Agni. Agni is the god of the fire, who is born and dies like the sun, but is also the spirit of sacrifice. Sometimes he is prayed to for simple acts, like the kindling of a fire; sometimes his birth and death are the great riddle in which all of life is wrapped up.

Soma is the opposite of Agni, but also his partner. In a word, Soma is water: rain, fertility, plenty. As Agni is to the sun, so is Soma to the moon, and the night. Sometimes, in opposition to Agni, Soma is female, but sometimes a potent male animal, a bull or a horse. Without Soma, the universe would be nothing but a chaos of fire: it's Soma which nourishes it and gives it substance. Without Agni, the universe would be cold and dead. The struggle between Agni and Soma is one of violent conflict, but is also where the essence of life is generated. When Soma and Agni unite, the result is satya — the ultimate truth about nature and the cosmos.

But Soma has an incarnation here on earth, just as Agni can be incarnated in fire. Soma is a god, but *soma* is a plant: a particular plant, a unique plant, the Plant of the Gods. The *soma* plant is the only object in creation where the divine principle of Soma is fully expressed: in form it may be merely a plant, but in its true nature it's the quintessence of the celestial realm where only the gods live. The *soma* plant can be prepared and its essence drunk, and it takes everyone who drinks it to the same place.

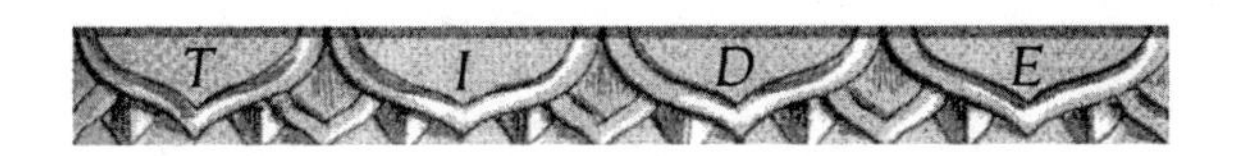

The *Rig Veda* is full of poetic descriptions of *soma* intoxication, all trying to out-do each other in splendour and cosmic imagery. The poets beg to be taken to the world of *soma*: *"Where the inextinguishable light shines, the world where the sun was placed, in that immortal, unfading world, O Purifier, place me!"* They search for words to describe the new vistas which it opens up: *"I have tasted the sweet drink of life...when you penetrate inside, you will know no limits!"* And they even boast of their past *soma* ecstasies, in which they become all-powerful gods: *"In my vastness, I surpassed the sky and this vast earth — have I not drunk Soma? Yes! I will place the earth here, or perhaps there — have I not drunk Soma?"*

But, beside the soaring ecstasies of *soma*, the *Rig Veda* gives a great deal of more practical detail about the form in which it was drunk and the rituals which accompanied its use. The *soma* plant is pressed between stones, until its fibres have released the god within it. It is then mixed into a liquid, whereby the spirit of the liquid, sacred to Soma, draws out the god from the crushed plant. The pressing-stones and the *soma*-bowl are both sacred objects, and the ceremony is presided over by a priest, sometimes referred to in the later Vedic hymns as a Brahmin, the original priest-class from whom the modern Brahmins claim descent.

The poetry of the *Rig Veda* tells us much about the nature and preparation of *soma*, but these sections of the hymns are still highly poetic, and must be read carefully. For example, the process of making *ghi,* or clarified butter, is also invested with the spirit of Soma, and the two are often described together; *ghi* also describes the clear, purified joy in the poet's heart, and by extension the experience of drinking *soma*. In other hymns the pressing-stones and liquid are evoked to describe the sensation of making love, being attacked by a wild beast, or the way in which the river flows into the sea. Like much oral song and poetry, the *Rig Veda* is incredibly complex. Almost everything is a metaphor, often several metaphors at the same time. Different rhythms signify the role of priests, warriors or other players in the drama. Acrostic rhymes are buried across verses with a subtlety which no modern ear could decode.

So the *Rig Veda* is both very specific about the identity of *soma*, and very vague. At times, the preparation of *soma* is almost detailed like a modern recipe-book; at other times, *soma* is anything and everything. But the *soma* hymns give us a vivid picture of the spirit of the plant: it imparts bliss, vision, an earth-shattering awareness of the immensity of cosmic space in which the *soma*-drinker runs free.

The spirit of *soma* is frequently expressed in the form of Indra, the king of all the Vedic divinities and the patron god of the Vedic people. Indra is a god, but also a man: in many ways, he's the spirit of the new man whose emergence caused the Vedic culture to develop. He was born mortal, but "as soon as born surpassed the gods in power." His litany of achievements expresses the ways in which man, previously a mere animal, has gradually become like a god. It was he who first freed the cattle from the cave of Vala, allowing men to become cattle-herders; it was he who "produces fire between two rocks," the Prometheus who brought fire into the world, and with it cooking, smelting and metal-casting. And it was he who first drank *soma*, and allowed men to experience first-hand the realm of the gods.

This trinity of new powers — cattle, fire, *soma* — are Indra's contribution from the gods, but he retains a strong human dimension. He's a warrior, a hero, impetuous, brave, sometimes demonstrative and boastful, often so impulsive that he stores up trouble for himself in the future. He loves the intensity of the moment, fighting, chasing, running, making love — or, more than anything else, drinking *soma*. *Soma* makes him boundless in his joy, generous to all, the companion of all who join him in its Other World, fearlessly exploring a universe without boundaries. *Soma* is most often drunk with a prayer to him: *"O drop of Soma, flow for Indra."*

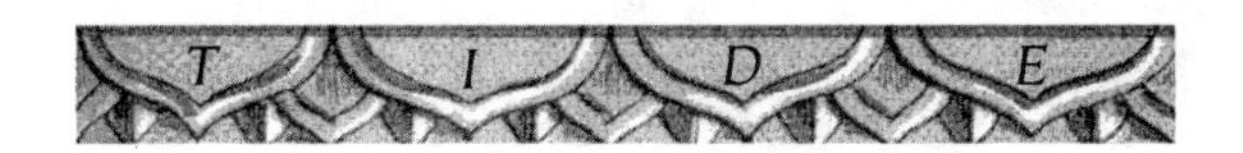

The time of the *Rig Veda* is consciously celebrated as a Golden Age, with an elegiac tone which makes it seem as though it may even have been disintegrating as the hymns were first committed to writing. Although they depict a stable, complex society in which various tribes co-exist and mingle, this was a world which was soon to collapse, leaving little but the *Rig Veda* behind.

And when paradise was lost, so was *soma*. Sometime around 2000BC, an economic collapse seems to have spread across Western Asia. It may have been caused by the growth of new civilisations to the West — tin mining, for example, becoming more prolific in Anatolia or Mycenean Greece, and the wealth of the world ebbing towards the Mediterranean. But, whatever the cause, the stability of Vedic society was lost. A time of migration ensued, with many people returning to nomadism, waves of invasion and warfare, the fracturing of the ties which had held the "five tribes" of the Vedic people together.

During this time of troubles, even the gods fell apart. The worship of the great divinities, Agni and Soma, was replaced with more fragmented, ethnic or tribally-based cults. The caste system was forged, dividing the people into 'Arya' ("nobility") and 'Sura' ("vassals"), ideas which are either obscure or absent in the Rig Veda. The Brahmin emerged as a hereditary class of priests and law-givers. Vishnu, originally an aspect of Indra, became a powerful figure in the new pantheon, but Indra himself failed to survive. His human qualities seem to have counted against him: he came to seem somehow too human, too prone to indignity, the butt of too many jokes, not really a proper god at all.

But, as the Hindu edifice emerged, another tradition was developing alongside it. The *Rig Veda* mentions a group of people called the *keshin,* or "long-haired ascetics," who drink a potion which brings them into the world of the god Rudra. They're described vividly: *"Long-hair holds fire, holds the drug, holds sky and earth...these ascetics, swathed in wind, put dirty red rags on. When gods enter them, they ride with the rush of the wind."* These ragged, long-haired ascetics seem to be the first yogis or saddhus, individuals developing their own spiritual disciplines outside the priestly dominion.

But these *keshin* are not *soma*-drinkers. The potion they use to transport themselves is referred to in the *Rig Veda* not as *soma* but as *visha,* a word meaning 'poison' or 'drug'. After the end of the Vedic period, Rudra becomes more commonly referred to as Shiva. And the devotees of the ancient Shiva cult of ecstasy are well-known to use cannabis, in the liquid form of *bhang,* as their sacred intoxicant. Early statues of Shiva associate him with the cannabis plant and the chillum pipe. Within the yogic tradition, it is commonly held that the yogic postures, breathing and spiritual exercises have their roots in the original ecstasies of *soma* or *visha;* the Vedic account of *"riding the gods with the rush of the wind"* comes to represent the disciplines of breath techniques rather than the use of plant intoxicants.

But, if we can conclude that the *visha* of the Veda is likely to have been cannabis, the botanical identity of *soma* has no such common-sense solution. The knowledge of the plant doesn't seem to have survived the breakdown of the Vedic culture, and the *soma* rites which were held by the later Brahmins were performed with non-intoxicating substitutes. Today, there is no consensus about which plant it was that provided the elixir of the gods. It remains one of the great unsolved mysteries of the ancient world.

This is the story of how I became drawn into the search for the plant which was *soma*. To start with, *soma* was simply a name with which I was vaguely familiar, mostly from Aldous

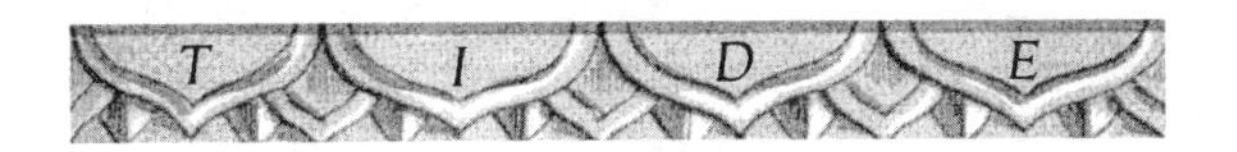

Huxley's use of it in *Brave New World.* I think I'd probably known at some point that Huxley had taken the name from some ancient or classical source.

I didn't set out to try to solve an ancient mystery. I simply found a huge number of disparate researches leading back to *soma,* and combining to assemble a partial jigsaw which it became incresingly tempting to try and fill in. My attempts to do so led me down a bewildering variety of different avenues: the role of plant drugs in the earliest religions, the pervasive role of psychedelic plants through history and across cultures' the latest neurological discoveries about the effects of these plant substances on the mind. They led me to make my own experiments with many of these plants, and to open up regions of the mind which I never knew existed. And, eventually, it led me to the high Indus Valley in the Himalayas, the original home of *soma*.

But, in retrospect, all this started before I was consciously looking for *soma* at all.

1

Telepathine

Leo and I are perched on the citadel above Urfa, in South-East Turkey. Below us, the city is still in the morning heat, sporadic babble in Turkish, Kurdish and Arabic floating up over the chug of traffic. Urfa occupies a cleft in the low hills which recede into the haze of the Mesopotamian desert. Dusty *'tells'* — the mounds of ancient villages — dot its flat surface, receding over the Syrian border to the horizon.

Two Babylonian columns rise up above us on the citadel, their carved sandstone pitted with age. They are known locally as the Pillars of Nimrod. No-one seems to know how old they are. If you ask anyone here about anything that old, it's all "from Nimrod's time."

We are researching a filmscript set during the Crusades, and have scrupulously followed the Crusader routes to this point — east over the mountains of Anatolia, through the mountain-pass of the Syrian Gates, down to Antioch where the First Crusade was besieged for weeks before miraculously finding the Spear of Longinus — the Roman centurion who

pierced Christ's side — in the crypt beneath the church, and rallying to win the decisive battle en route to Jerusalem. After that, we turned east, following the route of the Italian bandit Tancred, who peeled off from the main Crusade to carve out his own kingdom here in the desert. This takes me across the Euphrates, and into Mesopotamia for the first time. We cross the river at sunset: an old man with a donkey-cart is crossing the other way, and he wanders across the carriageway to present me with a bunch of grapes.

Our high perch has the last remnants of Tancred's short-lived citadel scattered around it, reminding us of the 'Eagle's Nest' of the Assassins, or 'Hashishin,' the murderous Ismaili sect who play a pivotal role in our story. Our hero is a cynical Catalan mercenary who switches sides during a hostage exchange in the desert, and is indoctrinated by the Assassin leader, the Old Man of the Mountain, to be sent back to the Holy Land as an undercover hit-man. The indoctrination revolves around the famous story of the Old Man's 'Garden of Paradise,' where he would drug his new recruits and lead them into a garden hidden in his mountaintop fortress, where fountains and streams of milk and honey flowed, and houris danced and made love. Returning to consciousness, the recruits would be convinced they had visited paradise, and would obey the Old Man blindly, glad of the chance to die in his service and return there.

The "Drug of the Assassins" is, along with *soma*, probably the most celebrated and mysterious hallucinogenic drug in Oriental history and legend. In fact, the two will turn out to intertwine through history, botany and myth in ways which I hadn't suspected. But, unlike *soma*, the Assassin mystery is relatively modern in origin, and rather more susceptible to decoding with the standard tool-kit of history. The classic

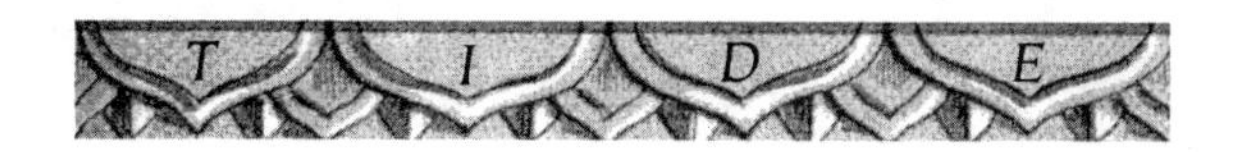

account of the Garden of Paradise comes from Marco Polo's account of his travels through northern Persia about a century after the fall of the Assassin order and has diffused far more vigorously through Europe than through the Arab world. Probably the roots of its popularity lie in the continuing Western inability to comprehend the loyalty of the Old Man's Shi'ite fidayeen, which enabled them, like their modern counterparts, to give up their lives without hesitation for their beliefs. Attributing this loyalty to 'brainwashing' with a 'drug' has always spared the Western mind the uncomfortable task of trying to imagine what else might lie behind it.

In fact, though, the Old Man's followers never referred to themselves as 'Assassins' or 'Hashishin'. They were Nizari Ismailis, and their founder, Hassan-i-Sabah, had originally been loyal to the breakaway Fatimid Caliphate in Cairo. The Fatimids were Shiites, renegade followers of the Prophet's bloodline through his daughter Fatima, and their caliphate was an Arab equivalent of the Anti-Pope in Avignon, a heretical order claiming the true inheritance of Islam. But Hassan split from the Fatimid Caliphate too, setting himself up in the remote mountains of Persia as an independent, piratical ruler, unique in the history of Islam. During the Crusades he played each side against the other, forming alliances with Crusaders and Saracens in turn, and keeping both at bay with the terror of sudden assassination by his suicidal elect.

Recent research has suggested that the names 'Assassin' and 'Hashishin' were applied to Hassan and his Nizari followers by their Arab neighbours. During the twelfth century, the mullahs of the Middle East tried to wage one of their sporadic and largely ineffectual Wars on Drugs, castigating the use of hashish as slovenly, low-class and contrary to the Prophet's *suras* against intoxication. The name *hashishin* became a generic term for lawless riff-raff, and was regularly applied to the castle-dwelling, supposedly godless brigands of the Old Man. In the following centuries, the word *'assassin'* passed into most European languages with its modern meaning derived from Marco Polo's distorted version of the surviving anti-Nizari propaganda.

But the more garbled Marco Polo's account of the Assassins, the more remarkable it seems that the legend should have become so deep-rooted in the West. And the more tempting it seems to try to tell it in a new way, one which expresses more accurately what may have been the truth behind it. Hashishin or not, it seems that Hassan and his Nizari were more than illiterate brigands. Their castle had a library which was rumoured to contain the most enlightened, progressive works in medieval Islam before it was looted and burned by Genghis Khan's grandson. They included astronomers, astrologers, alchemists, scientists and sufi mystics in their ranks. And their function as a 'secret society' does seem to have been built around a tightly-maintained core of spiritual initiation.

Just as the idea of a drug served as a literal explanation for these ideas in Marco Polo's time, it still seems attractive as a fictional metaphor for initiation through a combination of science and magic. But the main problem with the legend, we decide, is the image of hashish. In Renaissance Europe it may have seemed credible that a dose of hashish could turn anyone into a crazed dagger-wielding zombie. During the secret society panics of the nineteenth century, the hashish-crazed assassin (usually Jewish by this time) was a familiar spectre at the feast of paranoid monarchists. Even in the 1940s Harry Anslinger's US Narcotics Bureau was claiming that marijuana's main use was among criminals trying to render themselves more capable of acts of immoral violence. But the days are surely past where the hashish-crazed assassin will play credibly for a modern movie audience.

If not hashish, then what? Opium, of course, would also have been available — but what about something more intensely disorientating, more genuinely psychedelic? We begin to wonder: could there be a plant in Mesopotamia which produced an effect of this sort — like the psychedelic cacti and mushrooms of the Americas, perhaps? A shamanic path to the gods, suppressed by Islam, daringly institutionalised by the heretical Old Man after his split with the Fatimid Caliphate, when his sect became the first in the history of Islam to acknowledge no spiritual leader beyond himself?

We decide to dig into this question when we're back in London. True or not, it might work well for the movie.

☆ ☆

At this point a moustached Turk in dusty overalls saunters over to see what we're doing perched on a high outcrop of rock. He starts telling us about his life: he can only get casual jobs because he never learnt to read — quite an achievement in Turkey, where the literacy rate is generally higher than Britain. We tell him we're interested in the Pillars of Nimrod, and why they're so called.

"When Abraham came by this way," he tells us, "on his way from Ur to the Land of Canaan, Nimrod was king of this area. He decided Abraham was dangerous, and brought him up to this citadel, chaining him between these two pillars, and built a massive fire down below to cast him into."

We peer down over the precipice; below us, the whitewashed dome of an old mosque, with rows of colonnades spilling out into the surrounding gardens.

"But Abraham looked down over the raging fire, and caused the fire to be turned into water, and the logs into fish. You can still see them — the pool of sacred carp — in the gardens by the mosque. They've been there ever since Abraham's time."

We clamber down the citadel and find ourselves in the pleasure gardens. It's Sunday, and the place is filling up with families, slowly strolling and promenading around the paths.

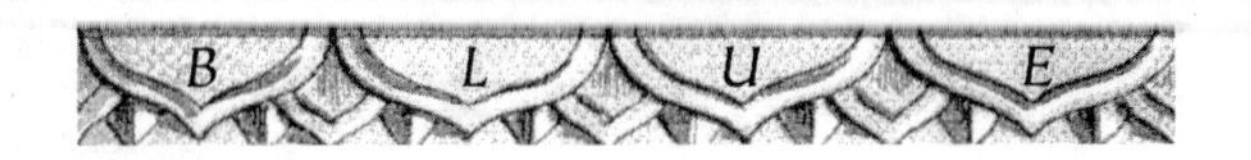

Young men sip hot, sweet tea at tables shaded by vines. Groups of robed women sit on the lawns in their private, set-apart areas. Armies of small boys offer to clean our shoes. People appear in the crowd who look quite alien to those of Western Turkey: timeless, flat, Eurasian faces, shaved bullet heads, nomadic-looking characters who wouldn't be out of place in Mongolia, or indeed riding with Genghis Khan. I remember Gurdjieff's stories from this part of the world, how when he was a small boy his father would recite him the Epic of Gilgamesh, the oldest narrative in history, just as his father had passed it down orally to him. Here, I'm almost inclined to believe it.

The crowd thickens as we enter the cloisters around the mosque, knotting itself at the archway which leads through to the pool. We make out the flash of green water, and its rippling reflection on the white walls.

The pool is shallow, rounded at the ends, a little like a small version of the Taj Mahal. The sun is fierce by now, and the expanse of water is deliciously cooling. Huge carp loll in the water. We sit at the edge of the pool, and watch families producing breadcrumbs, giving them to their smallest children to feed the fish.

Gradually, we notice that this is being done with more solemnity than, say, feeding ducks in an English park. People are making obeisance to the fish as they feed them, kneeling and touching their foreheads to the stone around the poolside. The fish are being worshipped.

Around the pool are small whitewashed chambers, fronted with elaborate wrought metal gates. Most of the gates are open, and families are paying tribute in these alcoves too. Piecing together the Arabic inscriptions, Leo figures that these are the shrines of local holy men and Sufi saints.

Of course, such cult of personality is technically forbidden by Islam. And neither of us can remember anything in the Koran which permits the worship of carp. The longer we sit by the poolside, the more obvious it becomes that we are in

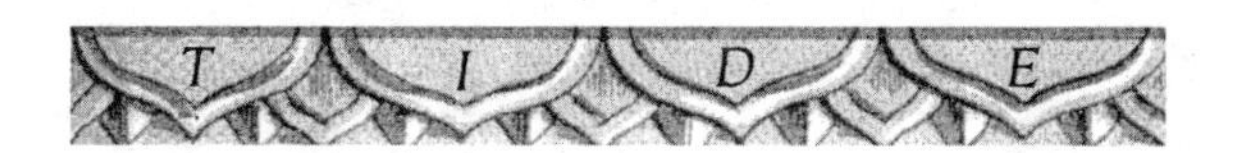

a place of great spiritual significance, and one which has been so for longer than the mosque has stood. Whatever the truth or otherwise of the Abraham and Nimrod story (which every local person we ask confirms without hesitation), it seems that, in this part of the world, Abraham's time and the present are linked more closely than we imagined.

At this point, my search for *soma* hadn't begun; but, in retrospect, it was this day in Urfa which sparked it: first, by deciding to research the psychedelic plants which might have been available to the Assassins, and second, by showing me so casually how much of antiquity has survived beneath the surface of the modern Islamic world.

Back in London, I begin to research the plant psychedelics of the Middle East and Central Asia. This turns out to be quite heavy going: there's no shortage of material on 'power plants' and their ritual use, but the Old World usually seems to merit little more than a footnote in comparison with the volumes of research on the Americas. It's here that the vast majority of power plant use survives: the mushrooms, cacti, vines, flowering trees and shrubs of Central and South America, and their continuing traditional use among the hundreds of indigenous American peoples.

There are various conflicting explanations for why the ritual use of plant psychedelics is so heavily skewed in favour of the New World. Some estimates suggest that there are seven or eight times as many psychoactive plants in the New World than the Old, but nobody's come up with any intrinsic botanical reason why this should be the case. Other sources suggest that the reason might not be botanical at all, but socio-historical: the centuries of more advanced civilisation in the Old World may simply have led to many of our traditional power plants being forgotten, much as the Indian use of peyote cactus and psilocybin mushrooms were effectively suppressed across great swathes of the Americas after the arrival of the Spanish conquistadors.

The Old World, indubitably, has two great power plants: cannabis and opium. Both of these have histories of use which recede far into the dawn of civilisation; both, more recently, have been introduced into the New World where their illegal traffic thrives. But, though both of them can have psychedelic or hallucinatory properties, neither of them are full-blown psychedelics in the sense that their function disengages us entirely from our normal world of sense-perception and projects us into the kind of fully-formed altered reality where, for example, an Old Man could convince us that we had entered Paradise.

Beyond these two, the most conspicuous Old World psychedelics are mushrooms. The most widespread are the various species of *psilocybin,* the "magic mushrooms" which grow across Europe and Asia in a multitude of forms, and whose ritual use in prehistory is attested by the rock-carvings found in the Tassili plateau of the once-fertile Algerian Sahara. Still prevalent across much of the Old World, too, is the legendary and distinctive *Amanita Muscaria,* the Fly Agaric, and its various *Amanita* relatives. But mushrooms are, of course, virtually unknown in deserts and across most of the now-Arab world: even the Arabic word for 'mushroom' is obscure and little-used.

The most immediately promising Old World psychedelic is *datura,* a genus of spiky, thorny shrubs often known as 'thornapples' which are widely distributed across the hot, dry regions of Africa, Asia and the Mediterranean as well as much of North and South America. Datura is legendary for its toxicity and bizarre deliriant effects: it contains a complex of organic chemical alkaloids, most notably scopolamine and atropine, which have been used throughout history as poison, deliriant and medicine. These days, they show up in dilute

form in pharmacies as over-the-counter sea-sickness tablets. Even a tiny dose elicits a strong physiological response: dry mouth, sweats, dizziness, blurred vision. Higher doses can lead to feverish visions and vivid hallucinations; the toxic dose is only slightly more, and produces amnesia, brain damage, heart attacks, coma and death.

In America, people like the Navajo and Zuni have developed a ritual around datura use, where individuals have a traditional framework for using the plant to generate visions of the Other World of the gods. In the Old World, though, there's little evidence of this kind of ritualised use of the plant to spiritual ends. The many accounts of its use tend, instead, to concentrate on its action as a deliriant or poison. The classical botanist Theophrastus gives the classic range of doses: a small amount makes the subject *"merely sportive,"* twice that dose gives him delusions; three times drives him permanently insane and four times kills him.

The plant has had many magical uses too, though typically connected with 'low magics' like sorcery and divination. According to a nineteenth-century account, Abyssinian sorcerers make people smoke datura leaves to produce unconsciousness and amnesia, filling in the gaps later on with supernatural events and prophecies of their own invention. A recurrent datura story in the deserts of the Middle East is that of datura being slipped into drink or food, and the victim being robbed while unconscious.

Interestingly enough, precisely this same story recently generated a full-scale mass panic in Colombia. *Burundanga,* a preparation made from the spectacular South American *brugmansia,* flowering trees related to the daturas, was implicated in a rash of unexplained kidnappings, robbery and murder which spread right across the country in 1993. Amnesiac victims in casualty wards found themselves robbed or raped; doctors attributed the crimes to the *"perfect chemical hypnosis"* of *burundanga.* A diplomat caught with two kilos of cocaine told police that he'd met a strange woman in a bar, entirely lost two days of memory and returned to consciousness in possession of the drugs. Doctors began to hypothesize about a new and especially virulent *burundanga,* synthesized in high-tech labs with benzodiazepines and other pharmaceutical ingredients.

Most interesting of all, this *burundanga* flap generated exactly the same story as the Assassin legend. Since the potion was also said to visit the subject with hypnotic suggestibility, it was believed possible to slip someone a drink and tell them to go and kill someone, which they would then accomplish with no recall of the event. Suddenly Colombia was rife with tales of 'brainwashed zombie assassins,' and people began refusing any food or drink offered them by strangers.

It could be argued from this that datura is a highly plausible Drug of the Assassins, since it still manifests the same effects halfway across the world. But my feeling is that this story actually demonstrates the opposite: that 'brainwashed zombie assassin' stories generate themselves for other, broader social and cultural reasons, and a scientific explanation is imposed retrospectively. In the United States, for example, the brainwashed zombie assassin has been a potent theme from the Cold War myth of the Manchurian Candidate through to today's complex of alien abduction and covert control conspiracies: here, though, the 'scientific explanation' which has grown up typically involves high-tech mind control — low-frequency or microwave radiation, for example — rather than a drug.

Probably the best-known visionary tales from the Old World come not from datura but from its chemical cousins, the other solanaceous plants like belladonna or Deadly Nightshade, mandrake and henbane. These 'hexing herbs' have always been traditionally associated with witchcraft, though it's still hard to assess how much they were actually used in early modern Europe, or how much of the witch craze's visions of Sabbats, broomsticks and animal shape-shifting were due to their chemical action. Modern historians like Norman Cohn have made it clear that many of the lurid confessions of witchcraft were cooked up by villagers and judges rather than the witches themselves, and thus probably reflect the prurient imaginations of the persecutors; but recent scholars such as Carlo Ginzburg have suggested that this devalues the imaginative content of the visions of the Sabbat, some of which may have originated in genuine accounts of visionary or shamanic techniques involving the 'hexing herbs'.

We certainly have contemporary recipes for 'flying ointments' which date back to the witch craze — in fact, Classical Greek accounts of witches' potions, like the one in Apuleius' *The Golden Ass,* suggest that the knowledge of the visionary use of these plants was a genuine inheritance from antiquity. Perhaps the classic sixteenth-century account is by Andres de Laguna, the physician to Philip II of Spain and one of the few extant sources of the time to attribute the visions of witches to their 'flying ointments'. He himself experimented with the ointment, which included hemlock, nightshade, henbane and mandrake, rubbing it on the skin of the wife of the public executioner of Metz. He noted her thirty-six-hour trance, from which she recovered with accounts of erotic and out-of-body dreams. It's one of the distinctive properties of these alkaloids that they can be absorbed through the skin: this has led to the modern supposition that the symbolic significance of the witch's 'flying broomstick' was that it was used to apply the salve to the highly absorbent skin of the vagina.

On reflection, though, I'm not sure that datura is the Drug of the Assassins which I'm looking for. There are undoubted similarities between many datura stories and the Assassin myth, but the similarities are typically in the underlying themes of paranoia and xenophobia which parallel Marco Polo's account, rather than in the vision of Paradise which may have existed beneath it. Datura does have visionary properties but is more accurately described as a toxic deliriant, producing an experience which is probably impossible to guide and control in a ritual context to produce a shared hallucination. Besides, the effects are highly unpleasant and hard to square with the ecstatic glimpses of Paradise which the Old Man was somehow able to offer. Even when mixed with hashish or opium, as is sometimes done in the Middle East, the effects of datura remain chaotic and amnesiac.

☆ ☆

A few years ago I was working on a film in the parched inland desert of Namibia. A few days into the shoot, a local crew member pointed out to me the spiny shrubs which were growing abundantly in the desert valleys and dry river-beds. He identified them as *malpitte,* the local name for datura, an Afrikaans word meaning "mad seeds." Gradually, the presence of datura in location after location developed into a kind of running theme, different departments eventually competing to sneak the *malpitte* plants into the fabric of as many shots as possible.

I was curious about the effects of this legendary power plant, and whether it was still used. I asked around the crew, most of whom were hard-bitten, desert-living, ex-army truck-drivers, characters who'd happily machete any sidewinders in their path and maintained themselves on sackfuls of Swazi marijuana. But even these fearless charcters drew the line at *malpitte.* A couple of them had witnessed the effects of the seeds on others: one remembered having to wrestle an axe off a *malpitte*-crazed buddy who'd subsequently gone into a coma. The unlikely message was Just Say No.

It's this, as much as anything else, which makes me sceptical about the visionary or ritual value of datura. The teeming and proliferating drug subcultures of the last thiry years provide a valuable new perspective on the history of

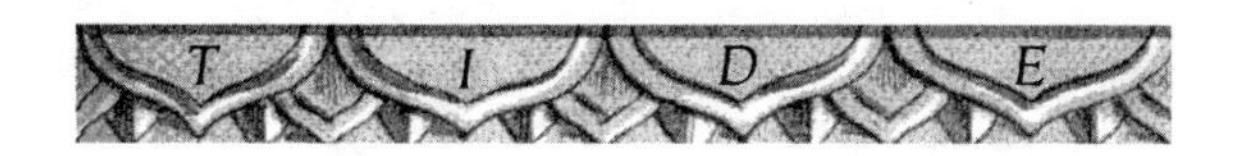

plant drugs: the curiosity, practical experimentation and gossip of millions of volunteer subjects can often tell us more than volumes of historical speculation. Psilocybin mushrooms, for example, were barely known in the West thirty years ago. Now, they're not only harvested eagerly every autumn across Europe and the States — there's even a thriving cottage industry of mail-order spores, sterile mason jars and accessories to grow them at home. Clearly, this is a high worth cultivating. Datura, by contrast, grows rampantly almost everywhere and remains entirely legal: if there was any pleasant or otherwise rewarding experience to be had from its consumption, we'd be likely to have heard a great deal more about it.

Eventually, however, I put the question to the most solid-gone member of the crew, a silent carpenter with a long beard called Hamid. He spent most of the time on his own, carving elaborate props which somehow never seemed to make it into the movie. Yes, he'd tried *malpitte*.

I expressed my surprise, after all the other reactions I'd had. Ah, he said, the mistake most people make is to eat the seeds. The seeds are full of bad *djinn,* drive you crazy, lose your mind so bad you never get it back. What you should do is go out into the middle of the desert on your own and smoke the leaves.

I ask him what happens.

"You feel as if you're in a box," he replies calmly.

I beg him to elaborate further, but he's returned to his carving, and to a world of his own.

I dig a little deeper into the Old World pharmacopeia, looking for a psychedelic plant which is less familiar: one limited to a specific region, perhaps, or associated with a culture long forgotten. Eventually I find another candidate: a high desert shrub called Syrian Rue. This isn't the best name

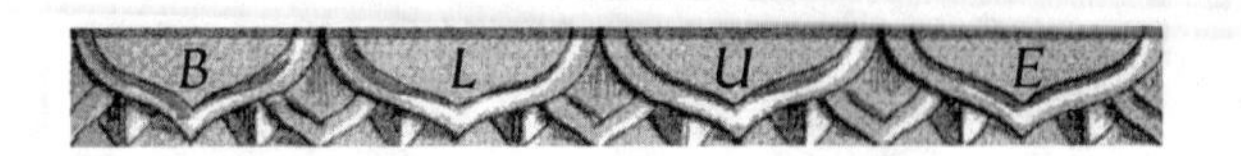

for it, since it's not really a rue and isn't by any means exclusive to Syria: in the West, it's often referred to by its Latin name, *Peganum Harmala,* which in turn is derived from its Arabic name *harmal*.

The psychoactive chemical in *harmal* was named after the plant itself, and is known as harmaline.

I've never encountered any mention of *harmal* before; but harmaline I'm familiar with, for two reasons. First, because it's an essential ingredient in one of the most remarkable and best-studied psychedelic plant brews from Amazon South America: *ayahuasca*.

Ayahuasca, the "vine of the soul," is the most fascinating and complex of all the South American plant hallucinogens. It's used, in various forms, by dozens of different tribal groups as a medicine, a purgative, a spiritual protector, a tool for divination and particularly as a ritual intoxicant which delivers the person who takes it to the Other World of the gods.

Ayahuasca is a liquid derived from the bark and leaves of various plants to produce an effect which wasn't remotely understood by Western medicine until recent times, and whose exact mechanism of action in the brain is still only vaguely understood. Many of the plants in the brew contain di-methyl tryptamine or DMT, a potent hallucinogen related to the psilocybin contained in mushrooms. But an essential constituent contained in all *ayahuasca* brews is the jungle vine *yage* (*Banisteriopsis Caapi*), which is the source of the harmaline.

Ayahuasca has been used in the Amazon since time immemorial, to judge by the pre-Columbian rock carvings which differ little from the traditional art produced by today's *ayahuasca*-drinkers. It first came to the notice of Western science in the 1850s, when the botanist Richard Spruce not only observed *ayahuasca* rites on the Rio Negro, but also sampled some of the brew itself. The only effect he records is that it made him extremely sick.

The full effects of *ayahuasca* were first experienced by

foreigners in the early years of this century. In 1907 a Brazilian rubber-tapper named Manuel Cordova-Rios was kidnapped by Indians in the upper reaches of the Rio Tigre. He lived with them for several years, during which time he was initiated into the world of the tribe. His final, most sacred initiation was by the traditional visionary method of the *ayahuasca* ritual.

The experiences he describes are extraordinary. After several days of strict dietary control by the older women of the tribe, he and the other men sat in a circle in the jungle and drank cups of *ayahuasca* while chanting in high falsetto voices. He soon found himself in a transformed world of rippling colours and shapes, where the forest itself seemed to be alive. Sparks of blue light flashed off the skin of a boa which glided slowly past the group.

The chief then directed the attention of the group to different birds and beasts of the forest. As he conjured each one up with its *icaro,* or specific chant, the forest creatures materialised one by one in the centre of the circle. The chief enumerated the characteristic markings, sounds and behaviours of each in turn, the privileged information sinking deeply into the minds of the participants.

Cordoba-Rios had the utterly convincing sensation that he was seeing exactly the same visions as the rest of the tribe, brought forth from the group mind by the action of the drug and the spiritual guidance of the chief. On one of his later trips he received startling confirmation of this feeling. Sometime before being captured by the tribe, he had been walking alone in the jungle and had encountered a black jaguar in his path. They had stared at each other for a tense moment, and the jaguar had slunk off into the forest. Now, during a subsequent *ayahuasca* session, the same black jaguar materialised in the middle of the group. All the members of the tribe plainly saw it too, looking up at Cordoba-Rios to acknowledge that this vision came from him. After the session, he was re-christened *ino moxo,* 'black jaguar'.

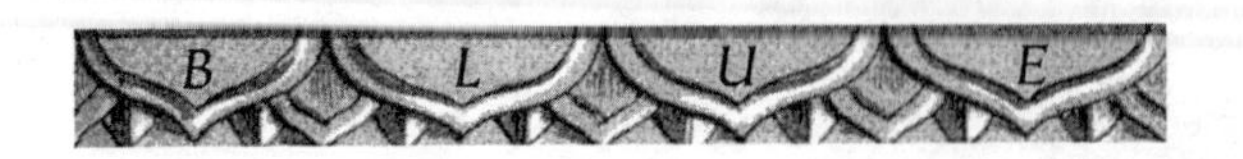

The telepathic qualities of *ayahuasca* were a common feature of the early Western accounts. Subjects reported similar visions, often the sensation of flying over cities, trees, parks or other elaborate landscapes. These landscapes always presented themselves as shared visions, ones which had been previously visited by other ayahuasceros or in which other people and entities could be contacted. In many Amazon cosmologies, the world visited with *ayahuasca* is the primordial world, an animist Garden of Eden where everything which is seen is the purest form of the landscape, creature or event, and the *ayahuasca*-drinker is present on the First Day of creation, witnessing the world in its original, pristine state.

Ayahuasca was first chemically analysed in the 1920s by a German chemist called Fischer. Isolating the active ingredient, he christened it *'telepathine'*. By the 1930s it was established that *telepathine* was chemically identical to harmaline, which had first been extracted from *harmal* in 1841 by another German chemist called Goebel. The name harmaline was standardised, and the plant extract was discovered to contain several closely-related alkaloids, which were given names including harmine, tetrahydroharmine and harmalan, and referred to collectively as beta-carbolines or 'harmala alkaloids'.

The next step in the understanding of the action of *ayahuasca* was one of the defining moments in the development of modern ethnobotany. Richard Evans Schultes, a Harvard botanist, made several trips to the Amazon in the 1950s and studied *ayahuasca* use with unprecedented sensitivity both to the conditions under which it was used and to the Indians' own account of what it did. As a result, he was able to publish through the Harvard Botanical Press the story of a plant drug which was prepared and consumed with levels of technical sophistication which had never previously been conceived, and which depended upon a level of theoretical chemistry so abstruse that it had baffled Western investigators for a century.

As Schultes himself put it, *"one wonders how people in primitive societies, with no knowledge of chemistry or physiology, ever hit upon the solution to the activation of an alkaloid by a monoamine oxidase inhibitor."*

Biochemistry isn't my strong suit. Fortunately, my friend Skip is a neuropharmacologist; fortunately, too, he's possessed of almost infinite patience. Over several evenings of repeated questioning, I assemble the basic pieces of the puzzle.

DMT and harmaline are loosely-related organic molecules. Harmaline can be absorbed through the stomach, and thus is active when drunk. DMT is inactive when swallowed, as it's broken down by our stomach enzymes: to have any effect, it has to be smoked, sniffed or injected. But it becomes activated when drunk in combination with harmaline: furthermore, this combination of the two chemicals creates a brew which has very different effects from either of them alone.

The basis of this interaction is the principle which Schultes identified: monoamine oxidase inhibition. Monoamine oxidase is the enzyme which breaks down many organic molecules in the body, including DMT and harmaline. But the action of both DMT and harmaline is to inhibit the production of this enzyme, increasing and prolonging the effect of both drugs as the depleted enzyme struggles to break both compounds down simultaneously. Not only does the combination allow the DMT to remain active in the first place, it also massively intensifies the effect of both.

Schultes found that a huge number of plants are used in different *ayahuasca* preparations, including dozens of varieties of the harmaline-containing *Banisteriopsis* vine. Although according to Western taxonomy there are only two species of this vine, the Indians recognise many different sub-species and cultivars, and also distinguish carefully between vines at different ages and sizes, and in different seasons. All the varieties of the vine are understood to have different effects, and are used in different ritual contexts and for different purposes. The chemical basis of these distinctions is still largely beyond us: more than anything else, *ayahuasca* reveals the bluntness of Western science's tools for classifying and understanding the traditional use of plant psychedelics.

☆ ☆

On one of his trips to South America in the 1950s, Schultes ran into a pale, unhealthy-looking American who was also looking for *ayahuasca*, or *yage*, the name by which it had been brought to his attention. His motives were very different from Schultes': he was a veteran drug user who was looking for "the ultimate fix," and had heard that *yage* was it. He was an unpublished writer called William Burroughs.

Burroughs had become a heroin addict in New York, his life revolving for many years around a habit of mind-numbing prescription opiates, uppers and downers which he felt had desensitised his mind and body and which he wanted to stop using. But he still believed that drugs had the potential to offer an escape-hatch from the equally numbing and desensitising effects of modern life, and even a means of transcending the limits of the physical organism and entering a world of the creative imagination which was becoming less and less accessible in the modern world. He'd read some accounts of *ayahuasca* use, and had decided rather quixotically to venture into the jungle alone in search of it.

He recorded his expedition in the form of letters to his friend Allen Ginsberg, which were eventually published in the 1960s. Unsurprisingly, the general impression is a catalogue of misery: flies, heat, rip-offs, paranoia, junk sickness, dwindling funds. But he did eventually succeed in locating an *ayahuascero* in a remote jungle hut and sampling the brew.

Like most Westerners — and, indeed, almost anyone who drinks *ayahuasca* without the careful dietary prescriptions observed by the Indians — Burroughs found the potion extremely nauseous. Vomiting, dizziness, diarrhoeia and fainting made the experience something of an ordeal. But he did succeed in consuming enough of the foul brew to have a vision quite unlike anything he'd ever experienced before. As he wrote to Ginsberg:

"In two minutes a wave of dizziness swept over me and the hut began spinning...blue flashes passed in front of my eyes...the hut took on an archaic far Pacific look with Easter Island heads carved in the support posts. The assistant was outside lurking there with obvious intent to kill me. I was hit by sudden, violent nausea and rushed for the door..."

Despite the overall misery of the experience, Burroughs felt that *ayahuasca* had opened up a channel of transmission from which he would continue to receive other-worldly messages. Fragments of his visions continued to pepper his writing from *Naked Lunch* right through to his last works, with their obsessive themes and variations on his *yage* visions of *"the Composite City where all human potentials are spread out in a vast, silent market." Ayahuasca* also became the focus of his idea that, although drug addiction is a disease which reduces its host to an insect existence, it is also the shadow of an experience to which humanity was born but has subsequently lost. This dream coalesced for him, as for many others, around the *soma*-drinking Golden Age of the Vedas:

"I have heard that there was once a beneficent, non-habit-forming junk in India. It was called soma and is pictured as a beautiful blue tide. If soma ever existed the Pusher was there to monopolise it and bottle it and sell it and it turned into plain old-time JUNK."

The second reason why I'm familiar with *ayahuasca* is that I took it myself once: a memorable but inscrutable experience which left me with more questions than answers.

Years ago. Guy, an old friend from the nightclubs of post-punk Berlin, has just returned from a six-month stint in South America, clutching a handful of sticks of *ayahuasca* vine which he bought in a magic market in high Peru, between the bundles of coca leaf and the dried llama foetuses.

During his time in the western Amazon, he kept a keen eye out for a local *ayahuascero* to take him through the ritual. What he eventually found was Valentin, an Austrian herbalist who had set himself up as a local witch-doctor and was performing his version of the rites. For some reason, however, Valentin had incurred the wrath of a local brujo, who had supposedly cast the evil eye on him. This was driving him to paranoid distraction.

As a result, the *ayahuasca* ceremony he took Guy through was a confusing mix-and-match of Amazon Indian practices and New Age purification rituals. Guy's memories of it are hazy: drinking the potion, feeling nauseous, almost losing consciousness, being forced to sit up and chant *hare krishna* for hours. Despite the lack of jewelled visions and astral journeys, however, the chronic arthritis in Guy's knee seems to have gone into remission since the experiment.

Guy also witnessed the preparation of the vine sticks, which involved boiling, crushing and sieving them until they produced a sticky, bitter, black fluid. He's fairly confident that we can make the same potion again.

We go round to visit Richard and Immo in Chalk Farm. Richard, who has South American Indian ancestry, has long expressed a desire to try *ayahuasca*. Immo, with characteristic German thoroughness, sets a huge pot on the stove and begins to boil and pound the sticks. These are extrordinarily tough, and we return to the house for three successive days, extracting and reducing the mixture. Although it's only April, we decide that the appropriate place to take the brew would be outside, at night, around a fire, in the deepest wilderness we can find. Richard suggests a spot in Wales, beside a waterfall deep in the twisting valleys of the Brecon Beacons.

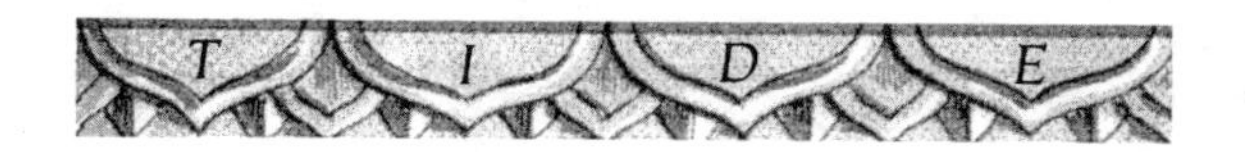

We decide to spend two days camping and fasting in preparation. By the time we've finished reducing the brew, it's produced about two pints of what looks like weak black coffee. Ideally it should be stronger and thicker, but we decide that enough is enough.

We drive to the nearest village and begin the long trek up the river valley. It's been raining solidly all week, and the steep river banks are mudslides interspersed with bare, wintry trees. Richard, a big fan of the Tarkovsky movie *Stalker,* is reluctant to lead us straight to the spot, preferring to introduce a random element into our navigation. We set off down a parallel river valley, eventually cutting across to the right river but finding ourselves on the wrong bank. The river is high and almost impossible to cross. We end up inching across a fallen tree onto a limestone outcrop in the middle of the swell, and picking our way across the crest of a waterfall. Guy slips, smashing the bottle of mescal in his rucksack and filling all his belongings with tequila and fine slivers of glass. We never find the worm.

It's stopped raining, but is bitterly cold. Progress is slow, as we frequently scale the slippery bank only to slide all the way back down it. Deep limestone chasms force us to retrace our route, leave the river bank and attempt to navigate from the next valley. Immo strides ahead, uncomplainingly hauling the tent and all the communal possessions, as well as dragging huge tree-trunks behind him for firewood.

By the time we reach the waterfall, we're entirely covered with mud. But the spot is beautiful. The river curves around a bend in the rock, roaring over a pitted limestone precipice, and forming a natural shelter in the elbow of its bend. A babble of voices seems to flow through the constant tumbling of the water.

That night we light a fire, and sip from a bottle of rum. Hunger gives way to a dull emptiness which begins to feel comfortable. The skies clear, and lightning flashes sporadically. The voices in the waterfall become clearer, until we are all

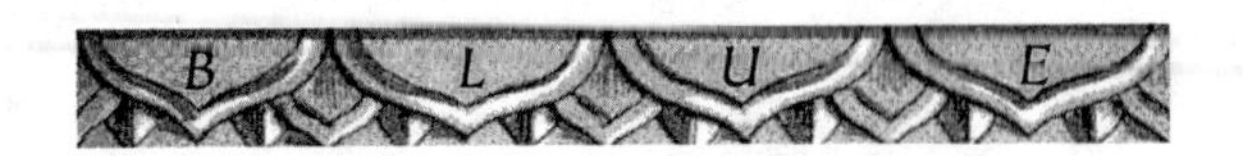

hearing them constantly. An intermittent rumbling sound drifts over from the next valley.

The next day we scatter across the valley, perching on rocks, watching the clouds, meditating calmly on what the evening will bring.

At sunset, we light the fire, and uncork the *ayahuasca* bottle. The liquid is slightly bitter, but not undrinkable. It could easily be a cold herbal tea. We pass it round in silence until it is finished.

The sky dims over the crags, the cloud cover sweeping across. Because of its steep sides, it's impossible to get in or out of the valley after dark. We are on our own.

We sit in silence, eyeing each other with curiosity. It begins to creep up on us that we have little idea of what we have just taken, and what its effects are likely to be.

Nothing happens.

After an hour or so, we begin to remark on this. We ask Guy how long it should take to feel the effects. He reckons we should be noticing something by now. The number of sticks was correct. Maybe the brew was too weak. Maybe we should have boiled them even longer.

We sit for another half-hour, our belief in this exotic potion ebbing by the minute.

Finally we all concede that nothing is going to happen. But we have a slight and rather desperate Plan B. I've gleaned the vague idea from my limited research on *ayahuasca* that the effect of the vine is often catalysed by the introduction of another chemical — something similar to psilocybin mushrooms. We've brought along a few sad, shrivelled specimens just in case: but very few. Only enough for half a dozen each, well below an active dose. What the hell. We chew them down anyway.

Ten minutes later, I begin to feel a numbness in the pit of my stomach. Not an uncomfortable feeling. A wave of tiredness flows over me. It occurs to me that I've spent the last two days clambering through mud, with no food and little sleep. The

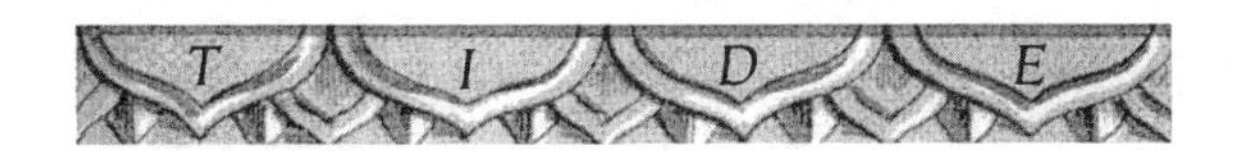

tension of waiting for the *ayahuasca* to take effect has worn off. I feel profoundly relaxed, and I sit down beside the campfire.

Raising my head to look up, I notice that Guy, Richard and Immo are also sprawled by the fire. They seem to have collapsed, like rag dolls.

"Feels like...made of lead..." I mutter. Immo musters a grunt of agreement. Richard and Guy are collapsed in a heap, unable to respond. I think about saying something else, but can't remember what I was talking about.

Gravity seems to have magnified a hundredfold. I'm drawn to the earth as if to a magnet. I lie flat on my back and close my eyes.

Wriggly turquoise patterns seethe against my eyelids. I imagine them as vines. They spark and fizz with bright blue flashes, like electric cables. They are extremely vivid, and dominate my perceptions entirely. My body is numb, its contours forgotten.

This goes on for hours.

Eventually I become aware of the cold, and decide to move into the tent. It's like trying to rouse myself from hypnosis: I feel there's no reason why I can't move, but now just isn't the right moment. When I finally summon the will to sit up, it's surprisingly easy. Everyone else is still comatose. I check that no-one's caught fire, stumble over to the tent and collapse.

The next morning, it's raining. We gather together our sodden gear and tramp back down river. We arrive just as the pub is opening for lunch. The Methodist couple who run it eye us with unconcealed horror. My stomach feels like a shrivelled walnut. I can't imagine eating, until the warmth thaws our insides out and we order the entire menu.

We confer for the first time about the *ayahuasca* trip. Everyone else's experiences are the same as mine, to the last detail. We all saw the same writhing blue shapes. Guy thought they were roots. Immo thought they were snakes. But the vision was undoubtedly shared.

Telepathine, indeed.

Since we'd exhausted Guy's supply of vine sticks, we never got another shot. Obviously we could have prepared a better mixture. Obviously we could have investigated the synergy with the mushrooms more thoroughly. Obviously we could have gleaned a thousand useful techniques from the accounts of the Amazon Indian rituals. But all this will have to wait.

As it turns out, it's waited many years, but comes back to me vividly as I begin to search the internet for references to *harmal* and harmaline. In contrast to the vacuous, content-free expanses of cyberspace which are the most heavily promoted by commerical interest, the drug forums constitute an example of the ways in which the internet can be a valuable resource. Semi-censored in the real world, drug discussions proliferate on the websites and newsgroups, where drug files, references and bibliographies are constantly keyed in by eager underground researchers. I've seen the same subjective report of a drug experience cross several continents and find itself cloned across dozens of sites within days.

In this case, this is exactly what I find. There seems to be a small, basic file on Syrian Rue a.k.a. *harmal* which pops up again and again in slightly edited forms, usually as a footnote to the burgeoning *ayahuasca* and DMT files which pump out the accounts of Burroughs and Ginsberg, Richard Schultes and the techno-shamanic guru Terence McKenna, to an obviously fascinated virtual public.

Its basic content seems to be: yes, this plant exists. Yes, it contains harmaline, in larger quantities than the *ayahuasca* vine: the seeds contain about 5% of the active ingredient by weight. It's still used in the Middle East today, both as a medicine and as a food dye.

Appended to the file in almost every case is a health warning: *harmal* is a monoamine oxidase inhibitor, or MAOI. This

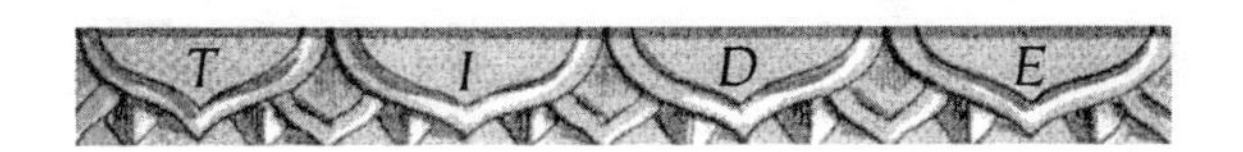

means that care must be taken not to combine it with certain foods: mature cheese, red wine, pickled fish, a whole long list.

This list will be familiar to anyone who's on a prescription drug which happens to be an MAOI: anti-depressents such as Nardil, for example. In fact, many substances are MAOIs — 'Sudafed'-type cough syrups containing pseudephedrine are an over-the-counter example. The foods on the 'banned' list are those which are high in MAO antagonists — substances which need to be broken down fast by the body's MAO enzymes to stop them becoming toxic. If the MAO enzymes are being deliberately tied up by the ingestion of harmaline or *ayahuasca,* these foods will proceed to break down into toxic enzymes like tyramine and octopamine, which will send blood pressure rocketing. If unchecked, this can theoretically lead to hypertensive crisis, even death.

Health warning noted.

Outside the twilight of the drug subculture, harmaline seems to have a straight day-job in mainstream science. My net search shows that it's commonly used as a chemical marker for clinical neuroscience work; it's also recently been proved to inhibit Pavlovian responses in rabbits. It's available in pure chemical form from lab suppliers, mostly without too much trouble. For some reason it's a Schedule 1 drug in Canada, but seems to have no special legal status anywhere else: we can only speculate on the possibility of some mass harmaline frenzy in Canada that the rest of us never heard about. The seeds are also illegal in California, where the plant is classified as a "noxious weed": apparently it thrives in the arid deserts of the American Southwest, where it was introduced at some time and for some purpose now forgotten. Another vague rumour which also circulates is that harmine was used as a 'truth serum' by German military scientists during World War II.

All of this is intriguing, but I still have many questions. Why, for example, if there's so much interest in and data on *ayahuasca,* is there so much vagueness surrounding *harmal* —

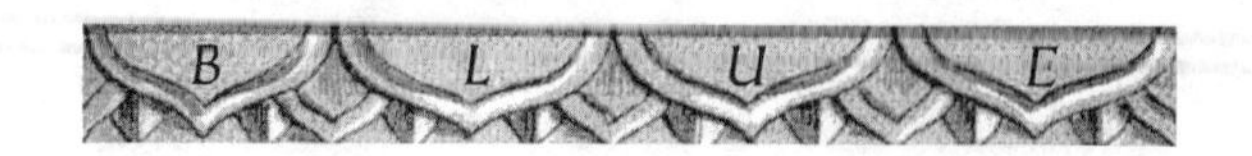

especially since it's a superior source of harmala alkaloids? Also, is it not strange that the same complex of plant alkaloids should occur in nature in two plants, one an Amazon jungle vine, the other a Western Asian desert shrub? And, since one of them is surrounded with the richest and most fascinating psychedelic drug culture on earth, shouldn't the other one be at least investigated?

Whatever, *harmal* certainly seems to be the most interesting contender for a fictional Drug of the Assassins. What particularly interests me is the specificity of the shared visions which it seems to induce: the writhing blue vines and snakes which I recall so clearly recur throughout the *ayahuasca* art and literature. The more specific the effects of a drug, the more credible it ritual use. It's hard to imagine a channelled spiritual journey on a deliriant or intoxicant like datura or, indeed, alcohol; but the wealth of ritual and structure surrounding the Amazonian use of *ayahuasca* suggests that it's possible to use the drug to take everyone involved to the same place.

The most concrete leitmotif of these specific effects seems to be the colour blue. I ask Skip how it's possible that a drug can make everyone who takes it see the same coloured visions. He tells me that, in its pure state, harmaline itself is essentially blue: when dissolved in alcohol, and especially under a UV light, it glows with a distinctive blue radiance.

Finally, in response to my various queries about *harmal* on internet newsgroups, I receive a response from a Harvard student. OK, he tells me, there is a scholarly work on the subject you're interested in. It's a monograph published by the Near Eastern Studies Department of the University of California Press. It's written by David Stophet Flattery and Martin Schwartz, and it's called *Haoma and Harmaline.*

Its main contention is that *harmal* was *soma*.

2
SOMA

It's this suggestion which leads me to look in detail at the mystery of what *soma* was, and the various plants with which it's been identified. The botanical identity of *soma* turns out to be a riddle with a complex history — a history in which, it turns out, several separate histories are wrapped up. It's the history of our modern understanding of the ancient world, and of the changing Western perceptions of the Oriental religions of antiquity. It's also the history of our progressively more sophisticated understanding of the nature and effects of drugs themselves. Altogether, it constitutes something of a litmus test for science itself, a question which stands tantalisingly poised on the frontiers of knowledge. Not only has there never been any consensus about which plant *soma* was, there's not even a clear consensus about whether it's the kind of question to which it's possible to know the answer.

Until recent times, to ask 'what plant was *soma*?' would have seemed like asking, for example, what were the chemical constituents of the 'ambrosia' which the Greek gods drank. The plants and potions of antiquity belonged in the world of myth, and it rarely occurred to scholars to take their identity seriously.

It's certainly true that many of of these plants and potions were never anything but mythical. A classic example can be found in the oldest narrative in Western literature, the Sumerian *Epic of Gilgamesh*. Gilgamesh, the hero, is grieving after the death of his friend Enkidu, and journeys to the land of Dilmun, "in the garden of the sun." Here, among other things, he learns the story of the Flood from its sole survivor, who also tells him that the only way to escape death himself is by finding the Plant of Immortality, a thorny shrub which grows underwater. Gilgamesh locates and plucks this prickly "mystery of the gods," but it's stolen by a snake which sloughs its skin and then disappears into the water.

Gilgamesh understands from this that unlike the snake, which can shed its skin, the lot of man is to die, and he reconciles himself painfully to his own mortality and eventual death. Even for him, the search for the Plant of Immortality is doomed to failure.

This episode of Gilgamesh echoes myths from many cultures about how death entered the world of men, and the motif of the plant is in this sense more literary than literal. But the search for *soma*, scholars gradually began to realise, is something else. *Soma*, too, is described as a 'plant of immortality,' but the ritual preparation of its use is clearly described and was obviously followed for centuries within a priestly tradition of ceremony and sacrifice.

This has become more significant as our understanding of the use of plant drugs in prehistory has become increasingly detailed. Opium, for example, has been reliably traced far back into the Stone Age. In southern Spain opium heads and seeds, buried with the dead, have been carbon-dated to at least 4000BC. Similar finds in Switzerland and across central Europe have confirmed not only that opium was systematically cultivated across centuries, but also that the

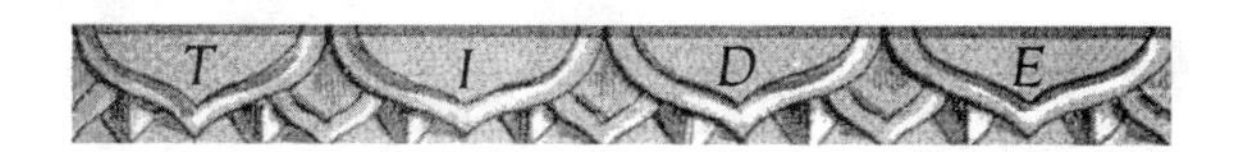

plant itself originated in Europe and only spread to its now-familiar Oriental habitat as a result of subsequent human traffic. Around the time of the fall of the Vedic culture, we find opium in Egypt, cited in medical texts like the Ebers Papyrus and used as a design model for poppyhead-shaped jugs.

Cannabis is also well-attested from the period before the Vedas, and perhaps more closely connected to them. From central Europe to the Caspian, decorated braziers dated to around 3000BC have been found containing charred cannabis seeds. These seem to represent the original method of cannabis consumption which the Greek chronicler Herodotus famously describes the Scythians indulging in in classical times: constructing a 'hemp tent' in which the leaves and buds were burnt on a brazier filled with hot stones, producing a sweat lodge filled with psychoactive smoke (*"The Scythians enjoy it so much they howl with pleasure."*). The nomadic people of Central Asia, to judge by the seed finds in their tombs, took this practice east with them; and these people may well have been among those who arrived in India at the beginning of the Vedic period.

One of the most striking effects of these discoveries has been radically to revise our ideas about the technological complexity of ancient drug use. Previously, it was assumed that 'primitive' people might munch the odd psychoactive plant, but not that drug-taking took a central role in ritual activity, and was correspondingly attended by complicated arrays of pipes, bowls, mortars, braziers and ceramic strainers, not to mention specific costumes, votive objects and other ritual paraphernalia. As a result, a whole range of finds previously labelled under the vague catch-all of "ritual objects" have subsequently been reidentified and fitted into the emerging complex of ritual drug-taking which extends across increasingly larger swathes of history and culture.

Clearly, this process has been aided by spectacular discoveries in other fields, such as Richard Schultes' ethnological work on *ayahuasca*. But it could also be inferred from the formal complexity of many casual drug-taking rituals which persist across the world today. In Africa, for example, the use of "bottle-tops" is widespread and common: people take an empty bottle, alternately heat and freeze the neck with aerosol and butane to snap it cleanly, then pack it with marijuana to form a chillum pipe. This seemingly complex procedure is in fact a process which perfectly satisfies the African taste for ingenuity, neatness and never having anything permanent when a disposable version will do.

There are plenty of even more baroque examples from the modern, technological drug subcultures of the West. College kids in America, for example, have found methods for slowly releasing and inhaling the nitrous oxide gas from whipped cream containers on supermarket shelves, leaving the cannisters half-full of unwhipped cream. This is equally expressive of the indigenous culture, demonstrating that the fact that the intoxication is immediate and free over-rides the obvious disadvantage of having to enjoy your brief high in a supermarket aisle.

Techniques such as these may seem bizarre and fantastically elaborate, but on closer consideration their complexity and diversity isn't really surprising. Drugs, after all, constitute an extremely direct way of changing mood and consciousness. A Martian observer would no doubt find the rituals surrounding, say, golf or haute cuisine far harder to understand than the Heath Robinson devices which, from the beginnings of human history, have so often accompanied the immediate and practical alteration of brain chemistry.

All this has a direct bearing on the history of the way in which the *soma* hymns of the *Rig Veda* have been read. While the carefully-described bowls, pressing-stones and straining-cloths were only regarded as incomprehensible "ritual objects,"

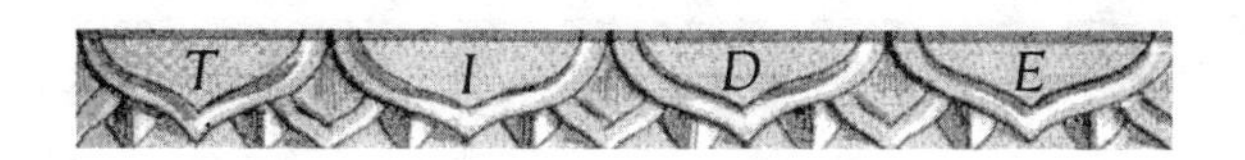

there was little chance of bringing the tools of modern science to bear on the problem. But before these tools could even begin their work, two other edifices of modern understanding had to be constructed: the Western appreciation of the traditions of the ancient East, and of the relationship between mind-altering drugs and the mind itself.

Modern interest both in the wisdom of the East and the identity of *soma* can ultimately be traced back to one man: Sir William Jones, a British judge in Calcutta in the 1790s. It was Jones who first established that Sanskrit, the language of the *Rig Veda,* was related to Greek and Latin — and, furthermore, that it was older, purer and 'closer to the source'.

This was the discovery which drastically and irreversibly altered the civilised West's attitude to the 'primitive' East. Western civilisation had been built on the Classical tradition of Greece and Rome: now it turned out that these were mere derivatives of the true Classical world, that of the East. India was transformed almost overnight from a nation of savages to a treasure-trove of ancient wisdom. Its ancient culture, particularly that of the Vedic period, was suddenly regarded as the key, not just to the origin of the Indian peoples, but of the Europeans. Since Sanskrit was now the root of the classical languages of Europe, 'their' prehistory was 'our' prehistory too. The ancient texts of India were widely read in Europe for the first time, and became influential on many modernist philosophies: Schopenhauer, for example, found that the cosmic fatalism of the *Upanishads* dovetailed remarkably with his own pessimism. In Germany and England, France and Italy, 'Orientalism' became an ever-growing field of academic study. Simultaneously spiritualism, which mushroomed throughout the nineteenth century, discovered its ancient roots in the Hindu doctrine of reincarnation, and the proto-New Age melange of theosophy and remodelled Eastern spirituality began its ascent to mass popular appeal.

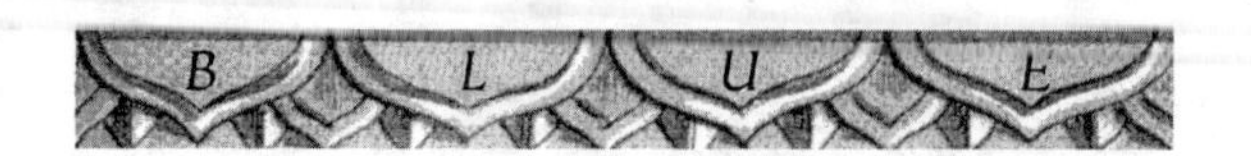

One of Jones' many massive achievements was to translate the core text of the later Brahminic code, the *Laws of Manu,* in which *soma* is referred to several times. In his version, he identifies the *soma* plant in his footnotes as *"the moon plant (a species of mountain rue)."* He gives no particular reason for this, but it stands as the first attempt at a botanical identity for *soma,* and one which would later be recognised as uniquely consistent with *harmal.*

In Jones' time, though, the botanical identity of *soma* was little more than a passing curiosity. But within a generation, a parallel obsession would develop with the nature and effects of drugs in general — and, between them, these two ideas would elevate *soma* to a *cause célèbre* of scholarly debate.

It was impossible for Europeans to become so inquisitive about the Orient without noticing the blatant presence of exotic drugs in these newly-discovered cultures. Furthermore, colonial ties — Britain with opium-growing India, France with hashish-producing Egypt — were making these substances more available for first-hand experimentation. The passion for personal investigation of drugs was dramatically popularised by Thomas de Quincey, whose *Confessions of An English Opium-Eater* became an enormous best-seller immediately on its publication in 1822.

De Quincey's work was groundbreaking in many ways which clearly establish its publication as the birth of modern drug literature. It was the first literary work to take a drug as its main subject-matter, though for much of the book it is De Quincey himself who is the true subject, refracted through the dark prism of opium. Unlike previous fictions, in which drugs are typically seen as magic potions which accomplish their effects regardless of the user's will, De Quincey's account is based on sound psychological principles. Opium, he points out, doesn't make you into someone you weren't already. *"The man who thinks of oxen will dream of oxen"*: opium won't supply an imagination where none existed before it was taken. In its complex portrait of the pleasures and pains of opium filtered through his own acutely-observed personality, he awoke nineteenth-century Europe to the potential of drugs to alter and enhance both sensation and character.

The other immediately recognisable trait of De Quincey's opium vision, besides its modernity, is its fascination with the East. His visions are spun from European threads of chinoiserie and arabesque; in his nightmares he is invariably transported to the ancient and evil realms of China, India or Egypt. He remains haunted by a Malay he claims to have encountered in the unlikely surroundings of the Lake District, where the two silently recognised their shared opium addiction; after that, the Malay returns again and again to haunt his nightmares:

"The Malay has been a fearful enemy for months. Every night, through his means, I have been transported into Asiatic scenery ...t housands of years I lived and was buried in stone coffins, with mummies and sphinxes, in narrow chambers at the heart of eternal pyramids. I was kissed, with cancerous kisses, by crocodiles, and was laid, confounded with all unutterable abortions, amongst reeds and Nilotic mud."

After De Quincey, drugs and the ancient East became inextricably linked, and the many accounts of opium and hashish use in the following decades would almost all inherit his basic tropes, including the idea that the dream world into which these drugs transport the user is an Orient of the mind, filled with amoral bliss and ecstatic cruelty.

It wasn't long before the drugs of the East came to the attention of science as well as literature. The French Orientalist Silvestre de Sacy had written a treatise on hashish use in 1809, in which he recorded travellers' accounts of both hemp and hashish. De Sacy was the first European to untangle many complex pieces of Oriental culture — the true history and

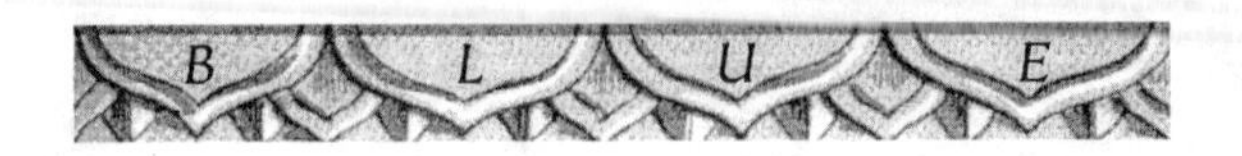

provenance of the Druzes, for example — but he was crucially defeated by the Assassins, on whom he wrote the first scholarly Western monograph. Their position as the ultimate heretics of medieval Islam meant that his only sources of knowledge about them were those written by their enemies. As a result, he swallowed the Assassin/Hashishin story whole. Unaware that they never referred to themselves as Assassins, but as Nizari Ismailis, he more or less confirmed Marco Polo's myth of the hashish-intoxicated fanatics as history.

But, in the process, De Sacy's accounts of hashish use brought the effects of the drug to the attention of the emerging discipline of psychology, in the person of a young doctor named Jacques-Joseph Moreau de Tours. Moreau de Tours was working under the pioneering French doctor Esquirol, who developed the diagnosis of 'mania'; when offered the chance to accompany one of the doctor's wealthy patients on a rest-cure to Egypt, he jumped at the chance. In Egypt, he set himself to solve a problem which was starting to come to the attention of the early psychologists: the comparative lack of mental illness in the Arab world compared to the more 'civilised' Europe. Moreau de Tours considered many possibilities — religion, race, climate — before focusing his attention on the Arab drug of choice, hashish, and the corresponding absence of alcohol.

In the course of his researches, Moreau de Tours became the prototype of the flamboyant-yet-undercover drug tourist. He darkened his skin and adopted local dress in order to infiltrate hashish ceremonies without attracting undue attention. He observed the rituals which accompanied hashish use, and became the first psychologist to self-experiment with mind-altering substances.

He liked what he found. He reported hashish to be safe, beneficent and far superior to alcohol: *"wine and liquors are a thousand times more dangerous."* Furthermore, he became convinced that hashish was a tool of incomparable value for the psychologist. On his return to France, he published his findings in a book entitled *Haschisch et l'Alienation Mentale* (*Hashish and Mental Illness*). Hashish, he claimed, should be used by every psychologist — not on the patient, but on the doctors themselves. The main problem with psychology is that it's impossible for the sane to understand the insane. But hashish enables the sane to visit the world of the insane — in the full glory of its delusions, *idées fixes,* errors of time and space, irresistable impulses and hallucinations — temporarily and with complete safety.

Moreau de Tours wasn't searching for the Elixir of the Gods. In fact, his hidden agenda was entirely rationalist. French psychology at the time was largely Catholic, equating madness with the Fall and insisting that sanity was a God-given state from which man should on no account depart. Moreau de Tours' point was that hashish demonstrates plainly that sanity and madness are not black and white, but that there is a gradual grey scale between them: a grey scale along which, with the aid of hashish, everyone can travel.

But although Moreau was using hashish to further the cause of rationalism, he quickly realised that it could no more be contained in the doctor's surgery in the 1840s than LSD would remain in the scientist's lab in the 1960s. He was interested in witnessing the effects of hashish not merely on insane minds, but on the minds of artists, musicians, writers, intellectuals, men of genius. The club that was formed for this purpose met in the Hotel Pimodan on the Île de St. Louis in Paris, and was called the Club Des Hachichins.

An evening at the Club Des Hachichins, as described by founder-member Theophile Gaultier, was a striking experience. As befitted a group named after both a mysterious Oriental drug and the ultimate secret society, the attendance was controlled and the admittance carried out with cloak-and-dagger theatrics. Moreau ("*Dr. X,*" in Gaultier's account), in Turkish dress, was the man who supplied the drug: a blob of greenish paste, the Arab preparation known as *dawamesc,* containing three or four grams of hashish: it was handed to each initiate with the admonition *"this will be subtracted from your share in Paradise."* The hashish was eaten with a light meal, after which the hallucinations began.

Few of the other Parisian Hashishin were as clinical in their interests as Moreau de Tours. Charles Baudelaire, an early member, was raging with his "thirst for the infinite," and in love with the gothic arabesques of De Quincey which he translated into French for the first time. He and his colleagues wrote widely on their experiences, and the Club Des Hashishin made irresistable press, becoming a legendary nexus of the romantic and decadent elite.

☆ ☆

In this climate of new Oriental scholarship and popular romantic fascination, *soma* became a progressively more potent image of the core of the mystery of the Orient, of the ancient world, of human origins themselves. As more and more scholars began to turn their attention to what it might actually have been, the search assumed the dimensions of a quest into the ultimate mysteries.

Unfortunately, Oriental scholarship began by tramping down a complete blind alley. In the late Brahminic and ayurvedic texts, written centuries after the 'loss' of the original *soma*, the tradition developed that the 'true' *soma* had been a form of creeper. Following this tradition, most early theories of *soma*'s identity clustered round the creepers of the *sarcostemma* family, a broad range of swallow-worts and milkweeds whose distinguishing characteristic is a milky sap, which was confidently proclaimed as the *soma*-juice.

Eventually the obvious disadvantage of this theory became apparent: that *sarcostemma*-juice has no mind-altering effect. This was dealt with by adding the psychoactive element most readily comprehensible to Western minds: alcohol. The idea which emerged was that *soma* had been a fermented spirit; along with this came the secondary theory that the 'loss' of *soma* had been occasioned by the migration to the Ganges, where the hot plains climate made strong drink less agreeable. Within this theory, the actual *soma* plant could have been virtually anything: suggestions ranged from grapes to euphorbia to rhubarb.

Throughout this fiercely-fought debate, trenchant criticisms were made of the alcohol theory: first, that *soma* is clearly described as being drunk immediately after pressing, which would allow no time for fermentation, and second, that alcoholic drinks are referred to throughout the Vedic literature as *sura,* and clearly distinguished from *soma* both in this and in the later traditions. But it was only in 1921 that a more plausible hypothesis was suggested: the Indian scholar Braja Lal Mukherjee claimed that *soma* must have been *bhang,* or cannabis. In the course of his argument he established clearly that *soma,* whatever it was, must have been both psychoactive and something other than alcohol, a contention which was gradually accepted. But his own identification of cannabis left many questions unanswered. For example, the *visha* drunk by the ascetic *keshin* presents a far stronger case for cannabis, and this in turn is clearly differentiated from *soma.* Also, if *soma* was cannabis, how can it have been 'lost' when cannabis use has remained widespread across India and uninterrupted to this day?

Mukherjee's *bhang* theory raised the level of debate about the identity of *soma,* but effectively stalled it in the process. It destroyed the previous theories, but left no consensus about a new solution, or even a clear idea of what might constitute one.

☆ ☆

In the meantime, the arts and literature had also worked the idea of *soma* through to a creative dead-end. By the end of the nineteenth century it had become one of the prime symbols of the primordial world of the ancients, and its resonance was frequently borrowed in fin-de-siecle clarion-calls for the renewal of the exhausted modern world by the rediscovery of our primal roots. In *The Birth of Tragedy,* Nietzsche's creative exploration of the chaotic Dionysiac rites which swirled behind the formal visage of Classical drama, he spoke confidently of *"the influence of the narcotic draught, of which the songs of all primitive men and peoples speak...as if the veil of Maya had been torn aside and were now merely fluttering in tatters before the mysterious primordial unity."* This scenario was imagined with gusto by the poet John Greenleaf Whittier, whose rollicking verse "The Brewing of *Soma*" conjures *"the scourger's keen delight of pain/the Dervish dance, the Orphic strain/the wild-haired Bacchant's yell/...the naked Santon, hashish-drunk/the cloister madness of the monk/the fakir's torture-show,"* and concludes *"we brew in many a Christian fane/the heathen Soma still!"*

By the beginning of this century, the name of *soma* was evocative enough for it to find its most famous home in popular literature: as the 'opium of the people' in Aldous Huxley's eugenic dystopia, *Brave New World.* But Huxley's wistful, ironic use of the term demonstrates the extent to which the previous generation's enthusiasm for Bacchic renewal had crumbled in the face of the twentieth century's evolving mechanisms of monolithic social control. In Huxley's future, *soma* has become a distant shadow of the elixir which once bound a Golden Age in its rituals — much as, another generation later, Burroughs' *'blue tide'* of beneficent *soma* has dwindled to *'plain old-fashioned junk.'*

The stalemate which resulted from the *bhang* theory of *soma* was not untypical of many areas of ancient studies at

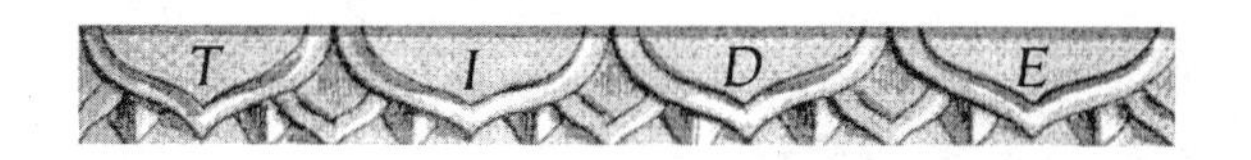

which modern scholarship threw all its tools in the nineteenth century, only to abandon it in the twentieth. Another example, also originally initiated by Sir William Jones' Sanskrit studies, was the search for the origin of language. Science, in these cases, tends to blame the subject rather than its own abilities, but in any event not to spend too long pondering its failure. *Soma* had simply proved too tough a nut to crack: the consensus became that we were probably talking about "some plant intoxicant," but it was impossible to be any more specific.

But a generation was emerging for whom the brush-off of "some plant intoxicant" wouldn't be allowed to remain unexplored. By the 1950s, a small but significant coterie of intellectuals was experimenting with psychedelics like mescaline and the recently-discovered LSD. Luminaries like Aldous Huxley were making huge claims for these drugs: not merely about their dramatic effects on consciousness, but about the influence which they must have had on culture and religion throughout history. *Soma* and its cousins, both historical and mythic, were back in the spotlight. Moreover, it was increasingly asserted, many ancient rites in which no drug use was actually mentioned might now be revised to include it.

The most famous controversy of this kind was over the Eleusinian Mysteries, into which most of the male population of Classical Athens were initiated over a period of more than a thousand years. It's one of the most remarkable aspects of classical culture that the vow of secrecy which accompanied this initiation was never broken; also the most powerful demonstration in history of the practical feasibility of a transgenerational secret society. It also, of course, leaves us with very little idea of what actually went on in the underground caverns beneath Eleusis where the ceremony took place.

Reading between the lines, and using other mystery cults as parameters, we can construct a vague idea of the proceedings. The initiate would have prepared with dietary restrictions, fasting and drinking from a sacramental cup called

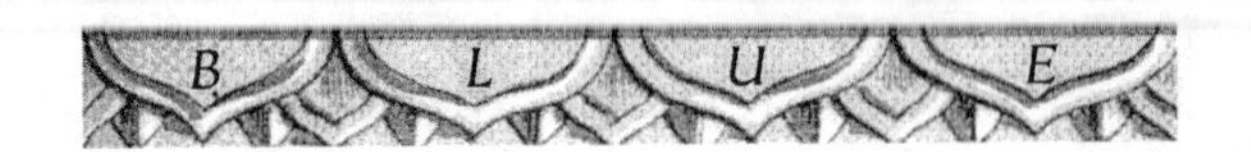

the *kykeon;* on entering the dark subterranean chamber, he would have undergone some symbolic death, perhaps being stripped of his clothes and judged by a god of the underworld. He would then have been bathed or cleaned, participated in a disorientating magical ceremony, and 'reborn' in new clothes before entering once more into the light.

The drug which was ingeniously worked into this scenario by various scholars including the classicist and poet Robert Graves was ergot, a mould which grows on rye and secretes a natural chemical equivalent of LSD. There were various planks to this argument. First, that the Classical materia medica, such as Dioscorides,' tell us that 'sleeping draughts' of opium, datura and other plant drugs dissolved in wine were in common use amongst the ancient Greeks. Second, that these draughts were used to stimulate dreams for those preparing for oracles and other forms of divination, demonstrating a religious context for drug use. Third, that the rites of Eleusis were sacred to Demeter, who was often represented by an ear of corn. Fourth, that ergotism — 'St. Anthony's Fire' — is a disease which has erupted frequently throughout history as a result of contaminated flour, causing hallucinations, mass panics and eventually severe gangrene-like symptoms. Ergotism is well-attested both in the classical and medieval worlds, and outbreaks have been recorded this century in Russia and France. As recently as 1951, the French village of Pont d'Esprit suffered an episode of ergot-inspired mass psychosis where hundreds of citizens are said to have gone mad in a single night, jumping into the Rhone while screaming that their heads were made of copper, or or claiming to be chased by "bandits with donkey's ears." Even the dogs are reported to have "ripped bark from the trees until their teeth fell out."

All these contentions were woven into a scenario whereby ergot, discovered in the course of wheat infections, was mixed into a potion with wine, barley and honey and administered to the initiates in the underground sanctum of the Mysteries.

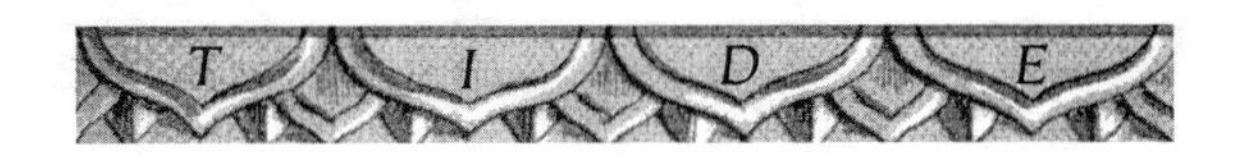

The detective work of Graves and his colleagues is fascinating, but their theory has little academic acceptance, and probably for sound reasons. The example of the Assassins has demonstrated how easy it is to impute drug use to secret societies — they must be up to something weird — and how hard it is to produce evidence to the contrary, given that the point about secret societies is that they're secret. Also, one of the things which makes the theory most attractive is probably something which also counts against it: the way in which it presents us with a contemporary model for understanding ancient ritual. Just because the modern mind would have difficulty achieving the suspension of disbelief required for such an initiation unless we were on drugs doesn't mean that the ancient Greeks must have been. Perhaps the closest contemporary comparison to the Eleusinian Mysteries is the Haj, or pilgrimage to Mecca, which all Muslims are urged to undergo at least once in their lives — a profoundly charged and life-changing event which is certainly accomplished without the use of drugs.

Perhaps the insertion of drugs into the blank spaces of the secret ritual tells us more about our own imaginations; perhaps, to put it another way, the Eleusinian Mysteries would actually be more bizarre and mysterious from our modern perspective if they *didn't* involve drugs. We can imagine that future generations might, in the same way, be tempted to interpolate psychedelic drugs into contemporary Masonic rituals: how else to explain that these self-important, upstanding members of society used to wear decorated bibs, recite occult formulae and bare their breasts for initiation? Perhaps, too, we can recognise a shadow of the Mysteries in our secular Western equivalents of the life-changing initiation: a recent TV compilation of interviews with actors who have undergone the intensely mystical ordeal of receiving an Oscar revealed that the majority of them have absolutely no memory of their sacred moment which is witnessed in close-up by billions. It would seem little more than common sense to

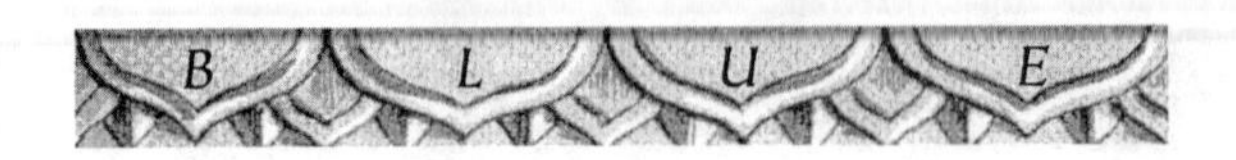

postulate the use of a powerful brainwashing drug to account for the otherwise unaccountable power of the event.

The ergot-and-Eleusis theory turned out to be the first of many modern revisionist hypotheses where drug use has been interpolated into almost every conceivable ancient practice: mystery cults and underground ceremonies from the subterranean Bronze Age bull-temples of Catal Huyuk to the Mithraic mystery ceremonies of Imperial Rome — not to mention Jesus' three days in the tomb — have all been redescribed as 'drug rituals'. While some of this is certainly possible, it also seems that there's a circular logic operating: these underground experiences would have been like drug experiences are for us, therefore they must have included drugs. The sheer volume of these theories, on one level, probably tells us something about ourselves: that our most recognisable modern framework for this type of programmable transcendental experience is, or has become, the use of psychedelic drugs.

From this perspective, it was only a matter of time before the burgeoning drug culture of the late twentieth century produced a new *soma* theory. But when it came, it was both entirely unexpected and from an entirely unexpected source. It emerged in 1968, in the form of a doorstop-sized tome entitled *Soma: Divine Mushroom of Immortality.*

☆ ☆

In the summer of 1927 Gordon Wasson, a Wall Street banker, went on holiday with his newly-married Russian wife Valentina to the Catskill mountains. While walking in the woods, he was horrified to see her picking mushrooms, calling them with delight by their Russian names and insisting on bringing them home for supper. Wasson, who had always been rather repelled by mushrooms, recalls his certainty that that she had picked poisonous ones by mistake and was

going to die. When she didn't, they settled down to discuss their cultural differences.

Wasson discoved that what he had assumed was a general fear of mushrooms and toadstools was, in fact, quite culturally specific. Anglo-Saxon people are what he began to call 'mycophobic,' regarding mushrooms as sinister and poisonous. So were the Ancient Greeks; so, too, are Celts and Scandinavians. Russians, however, are 'mycophilic,' like the French, Italians and many Mediterranean people: the Catalans, for instance, have over two hundred words for different types of mushroom. Wasson and Valentina began a survey of traditional mushroom use around the world, which soon led them to the pre-Columbian cultures of Mexico, whose religious art features a huge number of mushroom carvings, statues and motifs. They became convinced that, unnoticed by Westerners since the time of Cortez, the ancient mushroom rites of Mexico must still survive.

After many exploratory visits to Mexico, Wasson ran down a mushroom cult in the Mixeteco mountains in 1955. He was welcomed, seated among a group of Mixetecos dressed in their Sunday best, and given a cup of chocolate and six pairs of small *Stropharia* mushrooms, which precipitated him into a night of wild psychedelic visions. He wrote up the experience and sold it to *Life* magazine, who ran the piece to great international interest in 1957.

Wasson's discovery of contemporary Mexican mushroom use is the ethnobotanical equivalent of Schliemann's discovery of Troy: an amateur discovery of a crucial area of knowledge which the experts said couldn't exist. It demonstrated in a single stroke the improbable truth that, far from being stamped out by the Spanish conquest, sacred mushroom use had been continuing in the Americas for centuries completely unnoticed by Europeans. Shortly after the acclaimed *Life* piece, the Wassons produced the massive and magnificently-titled *Mushrooms, Russia and History,* a compendium of all their mycophobe/mycophile research, much of it based on linguistic

philology: the number of names for mushrooms in various languages, and the kinship between them.

By this stage, a big idea was building up an irrepressible head of steam in the Wassons' minds. Perhaps the core of transcendental wisdom in all ancient religions was based on mushroom use.

With this in mind, they were naturally drawn to the fountainhead of all Elixirs of the Gods: *soma*. Could *soma* have been a magic mushroom? Wasson combed through their files on Central Asian mushroom use, and located the most spectacular mushroom of them all: *Amanita Muscaria,* the fly agaric. Then he turned to the *Rig Veda*.

Wasson's *soma* theory was the first to be developed by someone with a good knowledge of many of the various and complex tools of ethnobotany. Having experienced a mushroom rite in Mexico, he was aware of the many ways in which it manifested itself: in art, in song, in language, in the seasonal migration patterns on which tribes like the Huichol embark on annual harvests to far-flung areas where the plants of power grow. Combining textual scholarship, botany and ritual ethnography, he found two main points which supported his theory.

The first was that, while fly agaric mushrooms aren't indigenous to India, they can be found in the high beech forests of the Himalayan foothills. And it's in the high mountains where tradition has consistently located the source of the original *soma*.

The second point was brilliantly conceived in that, if sustained, it would constitute incontrovertible evidence that *soma* was the fly agaric. It was based primarily on a single line in the *Rig Veda,* where the poet sings: *"Butter and milk are milked from the living cloud; the navel of Order, the ambrosia, is born. Together those who bring fine gifts satisfy him; the swollen men piss down the fluid set in motion."*

The reference to *soma* being *'pissed down'* was Wasson's trump card. The fly agaric has a very complex chemical action,

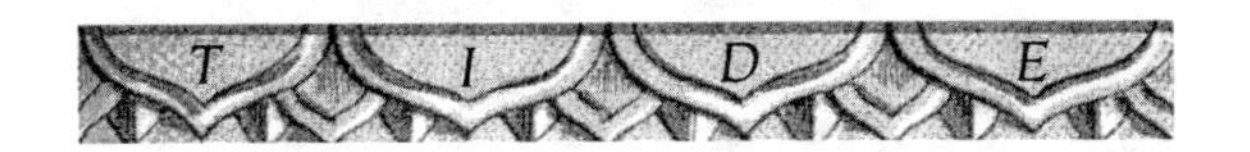

perhaps second only to *ayahuasca* in its organic alchemy. It contains at least three active ingredients: muscarine, muscimol and ibotenic acid. The proportion of these alkaloids changes dramatically as the mushroom matures through the season, or after it's dried. Furthermore, they all have very different effects, ranging from powerful stimulation to comatose stupor. Some are more toxic than others, making the effects of fly agaric dangerously unpredictable.

But the other distinctive feature of these alkaloids is that they are present in the urine of fly agaric eaters; not only that, but many of the toxins are filtered out by the kidneys. In traditional fly agaric use among the Siberian and Lap people, it's common to drink your own urine after ingesting fly agaric, to drink the urine of another mushroom eater, or even to drink the urine of reindeer which have eaten the plant. This is frequently maintained to produce an effect which is cleaner and stronger than that of the original mushroom.

Wasson buttressed up this verse with a great deal of material about fly agaric use in northern Asia, and also with many citations of Indian traditions of urine-drinking. The mushroom, he submits, was there; the ritual use of the mushroom was there; and the remnants of the tradition survive today.

In the public debate, Wasson's *soma* hypothesis came to stand or fall on the plausibility of his interpretation of the urine-drinking verse. While some scholars were convinced, many were not.

The first problem is that the verse in question may well not refer to literal urine-drinking at all. As usual, there are many layers of metaphor and tradition accreted in the hymn: it starts, after all, with the image of butter and milk raining down from the clouds. Soma, god of water, rain and the ocean, is seen purifying the earth with cleansing rain. The 'swollen men,' in this sense, are the clouds, pissing the dew of heaven onto the earth. The 'men milking the clouds' are not humans, but symbols of the marriage of male and female which produces the 'nectar of heaven'. Of course, this doesn't exclude a literal meaning, but it renders it less necessary. To make the point more crudely, there are not one but several places in the hymns where *soma* is compared to semen: by Wasson's own logic, it would be no less credible to assert that the Vedic priests must have been a caste of semen-drinkers.

With this clincing argument unproven, the rest of Wasson's theory becomes less convincing. Fly agaric use is certainly widespread among the indigenous people of Siberia and Lapland, but that's a long way from India; and, although fly agaric is widespread across Europe and Asia, it's rarely used as a psychedelic 'power plant'. Although its spectacular red-and-white cap has made it the archetypal toadstool, alluring and dangerous, it has traditionally been little used outside the Arctic areas where it's typically the only plant of intoxication. Even its name, and its reputation for killing flies, is based only on a few shreds of evidence from medieval Italy. Many classic references to its psychoactive effects may in fact be more accurately attributable to the far less conspicuous psilocybin mushrooms.

But, even considering the areas such as Siberia where fly agaric is used, it's hard to make a case for it as a plant with a sacred ritual use. Most Siberian accounts of its use are spectacularly profane. It's mostly used in orgies of intoxication, more like strong alcohol; in fact, its use in Siberia has declined with the availability of vodka. Fly agaric 'sessions' are revels which last for days, filled with roaring, laughter and drunken behaviour, and occasionally fuelled with further ingestions of urine undertaken amid much hilarity. There is a ritual use of fly agaric in the shamanic tradition, but this is undertaken by the shaman alone, as a tool to aid his 'ecstasy' or abandonment of his body, and to allow the oracles and spirits to take him over in a context much closer to what we might call possession or channelling than to the ritual sacrifice of *soma*. The great scholar of shamanism, Mircea Eliade, always insisted that fly agaric use was a late and decadent addition to shamanic practices, although he was generally reluctant to allow drug use any

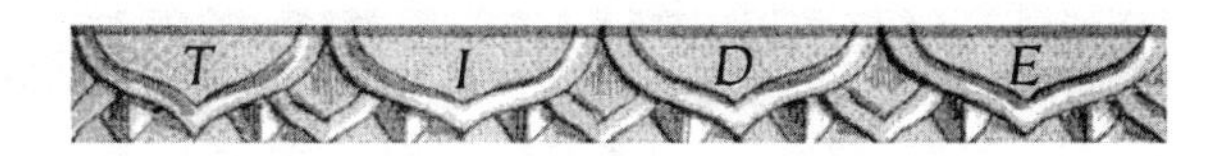

significant role in traditional magic; but, even allowing fly agaric the dignity of antiquity, the Siberian use provides no model for the type of priestly ritual which the *Rig Veda* describes.

Wasson's further arguments about the tradition of urine-drinking in India, without their surrounding props, become somewhat circular: urine-drinking is one of the mainstays of ayurvedic medicine, recommended for many different reasons and still practised today by millions of Indians, in ways that can be understood perfectly well without citing the *soma* ritual to explain them.

Another problem with fly agaric, as in the case of datura, is that the proof of the pudding is in the eating. Although identified botanically only recently, the psilocybin mushroom has become unquestionably the chosen mushroom of the recent psychedelic drug revival. By contrast, the conspicuous and widespread fly agaric remains very rarely used, its effects regarded by consensus as unpleasant, unpredicatable and unrewarding.

This is an objection which Wasson and his fellow-researchers, to their credit, took seriously and investigated thoroughly. In many ways, Wasson's most important contribution to the field was self-experimentation. Not only did he look at the question from every objective angle, he also made subjective tests of the fly agaric. While some scholars claimed that this made his work, in his own coined term, 'bemushroomed,' others saw it as an essential part of the process. It's one thing to speculate in ignorance on the what the effects of a drug might be; it's quite another thing to have taken the drug and visited its Other World. As Moreau de Tours, the first scientist to tread this path, wrote of hashish-eating over a century before:

"There is essentially only one valid approach to the study: observation, when not focused on the observer himself, touches only on appearances and can lead to grossly fallacious conclusions."

It was this principle which Wasson had followed doggedly from the moment when Valentina first showed that

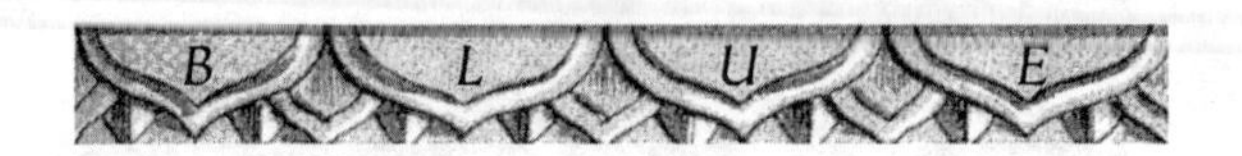

his fear of mushrooms was grounded in ignorance; it was this principle which had led him to his groundbreaking Mexican discoveries. But, in this crucial test, fly agaric failed to meet the challenge. Despite many experiments, Wasson never succeeded in feeling any effects other than nausea, dizziness, disorientation and lethargy. One of his colleagues had a single experience which he claimed was visionary and transcendental, but it was reached with a batch of mushrooms which seemed no different to any of the others and, despite many attempts, was never satisfactorily repeated.

Perhaps, in the end, the most telling objection to Wasson's theory is that he started out by knowing what he was looking for, and proceeded by arguing from his conclusions, assuming mushroom use wherever it was tenable and ignoring the pieces which didn't fit. But, mushrooms or not, Wasson succeeded brilliantly in lifting the level of debate about the identity of *soma*. The debate around his argument brought Vedic scholars, botanists, ethnographers, historians, doctors, chemists, poets and interested amateurs together, providing a model for examining the problem of *soma* which was far more robust than anything which had come before. A new benchmark had been set which any new *soma* contender would have to live up to.

3

HAOMA

As I work my way through the dauntingly vast literature on *soma*, it seems progressively more unlikely that anyone could suddenly have 'solved' this mystery on which the mighty edifice of Western scholarship seems to have so comprehensively beaten itself to death. But when I finally locate Flattery and Schwartz's monograph, I realise immediately that they do indeed have a new approach to the *soma* problem, and one which presents them with a mountain of new evidence. In essence, it's simple. They virtually ignore the *Rig Veda* altogether. Instead, they concentrate on the parallel tradition of Iran, and the ancient Iranian religion of Zoroastrianism.

Until about 2000 BC, the Iranians and Vedic Indians were the same people, sharing a language and culture usually referred to by scholars as 'Indo-Iranian'. Gradually they separated, geographically and culturally, and their traditions began to diverge. Their languages split off from one another but remained closely related, the Iranian version being known as Avestan after the *Avestas,* the Zoroastrian sacred books.

The Iranians had *soma* too, known by the name of *haoma* (pronounced 'horma'). Their traditions are very similar to the Vedic ones, but their ancient literature tells us many things which the Vedas don't. And, crucially, their story has a very different ending. Instead of the breakdown of the Vedic culture and the 'loss' of *soma*, their culture was transformed by their great prophet, Zoroaster, whose writings have survived unaltered and form the basis of a religion which still exists today.

Through the shared roots of the Indo-Iranians, we can reconstruct the bones of the Stone Age culture from which they emerged together, as nomads moving slowly eastwards across the centre of Asia. They were essentially animists, recognising the life-spirit in all things, which was known in Indo-Iranian as *manyu*. They worshipped sky and earth, but above all fire: the element which man had brought into the world, and which separated them from the rest of earthly life, giving them some of the attributes of gods. Fire gave them the ability to work metals from ore: copper and then tin, combined to make bronze.

By the period of which the Vedas speak, a pantheon of gods had developed, with a few differences between the Indians and Iranians but for the most part overlapping. Indra was a god to the Iranians, too — the hero of cattle-herders and warriors, the symbol of man's special relationship with the gods. Another central figure was Mithra, the god of the deal or contract, who was invoked whenever a bargain or a promise was made, the guardian of the underlying bond of trust between all the Indo-Iranian people. Mithra would survive for thousands of years, becoming almost unrecognisably altered in the process, eventually re-emerging as the official god of the Roman Empire, temples to him consecrated as far away as London.

But at the centre of the Iranian pantheon was the pair of opposites, fire and water, the same as Agni and Soma in the Vedas. Fire became the central religious motif among the still nomadic people: whenever they settled, for a night or for a season, lines would be drawn in the ground and a fire lit inside them to consecrate the spot and invite the god in to protect them.

And the spirit of water lived in haoma, which was sung about in similar terms to the Vedic *soma*: its intoxication was always accompanied by *"blissful righteousness."* It, too, was prepared by a priestly class, parallel to the early Brahmins: they were often referred to later as the Magi, the "wise men from the East" from whom the word 'magic' comes down to us. They presided over sacrifices, and the traditional 'sky burials' still practised by Zoroastrians where the corpses of the dead are exposed in a high place and devoured by vultures. But their main role in daily life was to prepare the *haoma* sacrament. This was done on a rectangle of cleared ground, where the *haoma* was crushed with a pestle and mortar. Beside it was a fire, a bowl of water and a sacrificed animal: all the elements were present, to enable the *haoma* to draw from them and give birth to the essence of creation.

The date at which Zoroaster was born into this world is much disputed by scholars but was probably around the time that the Vedic culture collapsed, 1500 or 1000BC. His homeland was somewhere in Central Asia, perhaps in what's now Turkmenistan. He was probably the son of a local family of some nobility, from which the Magi were often drawn, and we're told that his father was a priest who performed the *haoma* rite according to the ancient tradition. Zoroaster himself seems to have entered a priestly class of great diversity and sophistication where it was possible to seek out men of particular wisdom and develop a specialised path.

But Zoroaster went further than this. He built on the Iranian tradition, but expanded it from a system of tribal divinities into a universal religion. In doing so he became one of the very first humans who we know as an individual, and whose personal words have come down to us. He also became, along with perhaps Abraham or the renegade

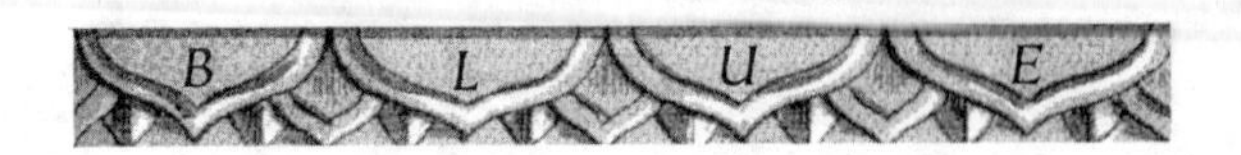

pharaoh Ahkenaten, the first monotheist, conceiving of a universe ruled by a single supreme God.

Zoroaster composed his insights in the form of poems which he added to throughout his life, and which became known as the *Gathas.* Like the *Vedas,* they were originally transmitted by word of mouth, and only written down centuries later. Like the Vedas, too, they are filled with rhythms, acrostics and patterns which demonstrate his audience's ability to listen to the spoken word with a level of understanding which can hardly conceive of; also, like the *Vedas,* they are filled with poetic metaphors and multiple meanings.

What was unique about Zoroaster was his ability to abstract the essence from the symbols of the Iranian religion, allowing individuals not merely to accept them by rote but to apply their own thinking and reason to them. Fire, for example, remained for him the central divinity of his people, but he added a layer of abstraction to it, showing how it also represented ideas of justice and truth. He elevated the spirit of wisdom, Ohrmazd, to the position of supreme deity, and showed how it produced a simple ethical code which all right-thinking people must follow: the triple wisdom of Good Thoughts, Good Words and Good Deeds. It was this abstraction which eventually allowed his religion to transcend its tribal roots and become the state religion of a vast and multi-racial Persian empire.

In elevating Ohrmazd to this supreme position, he also developed a new view of the universe: the cosmic struggle between good and evil which was to be so influential on Judaism, then Christianity, then Islam. Ohrmazd, wisdom and light, is locked in conflict with the lord of darkness and evil, Ahriman. This battle for our souls is not only the defining feature of our earthly incarnation, but of the life after death. Previously, the Indo-Iranian people had simply regarded life as the greatest blessing, and only conceived the absence of life as an eternal wandering in a dismal twilight underworld.

Zoroaster taught that, after death, they would spend eternity with one or the other: in heaven or in hell.

But this dramatic leap forward in human consciousness had a major casualty: the banning of *haoma*.

In the *Gathas,* Zoroaster's attitude to *haoma* isn't fully expressed, but there's a striking contrast between the legacy he inherited and the one he passed on. In Iranian legend, Zoroaster is seen as *haoma* incarnate: he is described as being *"created within a twig of haoma"* and born when his parents consumed the twig's extract — presumably a reference to his father's status as a *haoma* priest. But, after Zoroaster's time, the *haoma* rite was abandoned. Some time later, it was reintroduced, in the form of the Hom Yasht ceremony which still forms a part of Zoroastrian worship today; but the 'new' *haoma* was a non-intoxicating substitute, usually ephedra or pomegranate.

While still obscure, this gives us a great deal more to go on than the late, post-Vedic suggestions that *soma* was simply 'lost,' either through a break in priestly transmission or as a result of the plant itself dying out. It also gives us Vedic parallels: it seems likely that *soma* 'substitutes' were also being used before the real *soma* vanished.

The possibility which emerges from the loss of *soma/haoma* is that its use was deliberately abandoned, presumably by the priestly class, at a certain stage in the development of both religions. In the Vedic case, this process isn't recorded; in the Iranian story, we have some basis for inference. Zoroaster's newly-conceived religion enabled the priests to evolve into a more wide-ranging power-base than before. The new priests came to be the governing structure, not just of their own tribes and extended families, but of an empire. Their selection began to be political: priests were chosen from the most powerful families in such a way that all were represented equally.

The inference is that, in their original tribal setting, the Iranian priests were selected for their spiritual qualities, which

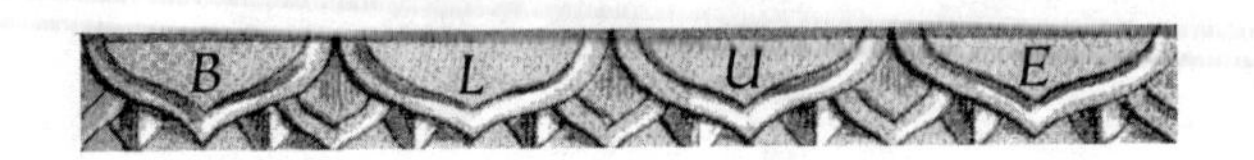

needed to be proved by ordeal and initiation. A priest needed, perhaps above all else, a mastery of the Other World of *haoma*, the strength to survive the onslaught of its blue tide and the spiritual wisdom to interpret its visions for the rest of the people. Once the appointment of priests became effectively political, this level of spiritual initiation was no longer a necessary criterion, perhaps not even a desirable one.

None of this is spelt out in Zoroaster's *Gathas*, but there are a couple of passages where it's clear that he regards *haoma* as a route to the old, false wisdom and not to the new dispensation of reason and progress. At one point, he refers to the "*wisdom-wasting drink*"; at another he asks:

"When, Wise One, shall humanity settle down in dwellings? When shall they throw out the filthy intoxicant? It is through it that the priests and the wicked rulers of the lands form their evil intellects."

It seems that, as well as the blessings of monotheism, Zoroaster also ushered in its curse: if the supreme deity is right, all other forms of worship must be wrong. Whereas previously they were merely foreign, the gods of another people, now the chosen people have the ultimate justification for abolishing them. Demons and evil spirits, once forces of nature, become the personifications of proscribed groups and 'demonised' practices: by the time of the *Vendidad*, the strict priestly code which evolved in the centuries after Zoroaster, the *haoma*-loving Indra has become the most evil of demons. If *haoma* was the sacrament which offered a direct, unmediated journey to the world of the gods, the very reason why it was so revered becomes the reason why its use must be suppressed.

This abandonment of the old Indic gods is still reflected in our language today. The Indian *devas* are gods; the Iranian *daevas* are demons. Hence the roots of these words which have come down to us include the senses both of good, such as 'divine,' and of evil, such as 'devil.'

It's perhaps not surprising that this struggle isn't recorded in Zoroaster's *Gathas*. His focus wasn't on the role of *haoma,* but rather on the new cosmos which he was constructing. By introducing notions of heaven and hell and the ultimate triumph of Ahura Mazda, he was also introducing a radically new version of time. Time, in the Indo-Iranian and indeed all previous traditions, had always been cyclical, a constant conflict between light and dark, fire and water, good and evil which mirrored the seasons on a cosmic scale. In a sense Zoroaster, by inventing heaven and hell, had also invented the future as we know it today — imbued with the idea of progress, forward movement towards an apocalypse when the laws of nature themselves will fundamentally change. This is the sense in which Nietzsche borrowed his name for his famous prophet 'Zarathustra': he was, in Nietzsche's phrase, *"the first individual with a sense of history."*

Given this revolution in consciousness, it's not surprising that Zoroaster should, by omission, marginalise the role of *haoma* in his teachings. There are suggestions that the *haoma* rite which he inherited had become somehow debased: a cruel, mindless ritual unnecessarily fixated on bloody cattle-sacrifice. But, in any case, *haoma* was the quintessential expression of the past, of the rule of the priests, rooted in the ancestral traditions of the Golden Age: in a sense, everything which he wished to leave behind in his quest for a new, progressive future.

But the Zoroastrian tradition and writings offer more than an interesting basis for speculation about the disappearance of *soma/haoma*: they also include many details which are relevant to its botanical identity. The plant is described much more fully than in the Vedas — tall, green and yellow, complete with twigs, stalks and leaves and producing a red-brown juice — making Wasson's fly agaric theory unsustainable, at least for *haoma*.

This level of description has led to a broader range of possible identifications for *haoma* than for *soma*. Cannabis has been suggested, usually on similar grounds to its identification with *soma*, i.e. that it's the most commonly used plant intoxicant in the area today. The shrub hom, or ephedra, has also been put forward: this is the substitute for *haoma* still used in the Hom Yasht ritual, and the case for it is basically that it's not a substitute but the original; ephedra, though, is a mild caffeine-like stimulant but emphatically not a psychedelic. In 1985 the Avestan scholar Gernot Windfuhr bizarrely suggested ginseng, despite the fact that it's even less psychoactive than ephedra and grows not in Central Asia but in China. Others have even suggested that it wasn't a plant at all, and that the *haoma*-pressing was a metaphor for the smelting of gold or silver ore, though this rather begs the question of why a metaphor would be couched in terms of detailed ritual and botanical descriptions.

The possibility that *harmal* might be *haoma* was mooted occasionally from as far back as the nineteenth century, but the case which Flattery and Schwartz assemble is spectacularly thorough. It has three basic planks: ethnological, chemical and linguistic.

First, they observe the extremely widespread use of *harmal* in modern Iran — not as a drug, but as an incense. Known today as *esfand*, its seeds are burnt as a remedy against the 'evil eye,' and to purify sacred spaces. This is particularly common in the Zoroastrian districts of the eastern cities of Yazd and Kerman, where the traditional fires have burnt continuously in the Zoroastrian temples for centuries. Like *haoma*, modern-day *harmal* or *esfand* is believed to originate from the mountains, to bring fertility and procreation, and to stand high in the ranks of magical plants.

Secondly, they note the psychedelic properties of harmaline as used in South American *ayahuasca* brews, and its

peculiar chemistry of being catalysed by other MAOIs. Looking at the Zoroastrian tradition, they discover that both the common *haoma* substitutes, ephedra and pomegranate, contain MAOIs. In other words, if taken with *harmal,* they would dramatically heighten its effects. And, if a non-psychoactive *haoma* substitute were introduced, the use of these plants on their own would preserve the ritual more or less intact while rendering the actual brew inactive.

Thirdly, and at great length, they analyse the epithets by which *haoma* was described in the Avestan tradition and compare them to those now used for *harmal.* The most common descriptive colour is yellow or gold, which is the predominant colour of the dried stalks of the *harmal* plant. *Haoma's* almost-obligatory epithet in the Avestan texts was *spanta,* meaning 'glorious' — the same word as *harmal's* modern Persian name *esfand.* They also note that *harmal's* name in virtually every Middle Eastern and Central Asian languages carries with it the memory of its visionary and magical properties. In Turkish it's known as *mahmur çiç,* or 'dreaming flower'; in Arabia as *mogannana* ("madness"); in Uzbek and across Central Asia by variants of *uzerlik* ("against the evil eye").

This strikes me as the most interesting identification of *soma/haoma* I've come across, largely because it involves a plant which seems to be a geniunely forgotten psychedelic. *Haoma* or not, Flattery and Schwartz's *harmal* story seems to pose a fascinating contradiction. On the one hand, it's the story of a plant whose visionary properties seem to have been known across huge swathes of the Old World, and which may even have been the plant psychedelic at the roots of much of European and Asian civilisation. On the other hand, its use as a psychedelic is, at least according to Flattery and Schwartz, long forgotten, concealed by a conspiracy of power-broking priests. Their account of its 'loss' is that the religious and cultural matrix in which *haoma* was used has been irretrievably broken down by Islam, under which power plants are no longer valued as sources of knowledge.

This strikes me as, at the least, an untidy loose end. I remember the carp-worship in Urfa: that must have survived nearly thirteen centuries of Islamic proclamations against idolatry. But, if *harmal* really was *haoma,* how come millions of people still burn it as an incense every day but nobody drinks it any more?

A few months later I'm in a Berber souk, in the dusty, aromatic heat of a small market town in the Moroccan Anti-Atlas. My sister Kate is watching in amazement as the owner of a spice-stall demonstrates a Tuareg lipstick — a chunk of soapy material which rubs transparently onto the skin, only to turn bright crimson when smoothed over with a finger. I'm squatting with the owner's son amongst piles of saffron, turmeric and cumin, looking at chunks of ambergris from the guts of sperm whales, blocks of musk from the glands of gazelles, wedges of crystalline sandalwood, a jar full of dried metallic-blue beetles, presumably Spanish Fly, which are apparently meant to be ground up and taken as an aphrodisiac.

We've spent a week in the mountains, January snow still on the high passes and the apple trees already in blossom, warm days and freezing nights. I figure there's a chance that *harmal* might grow this far west, and I keep an eye out for it on the high mountain plateaux, but no luck. In true ethnobotanical tradition, I've also brought a crumpled photocopy of a sketch of the plant. I show it to various friendly people, but no-one seems to recognise it.

Nevertheless, I decide to ask the spice-seller if he has any dried *harmal*. He looks surprised, scratches his head, repeats the name back to me to check he's understood my

French. He hasn't got any, but his friend might have. We go plunging through the souk until we find another spice stall. I pick the word *harmal* out of the Berber conversation. The new spice-seller nods, saunters to the back of his stall where piles of dusty plastic sweet-jars filled with herbs are stacked from the floor to the corrugated roof.

He produces a jar filled with tiny, rock-hard triangular seeds.

"*Harmal*. For what you want *harmal*?"

I tell him that a friend of mine in England is a chemist, and wants to analyse it. The truth, but not the whole truth. I ask him what it is that he sells it for.

"Oh, you know, a bit of this, a bit of that." He pauses politely. "A little medicine. A little magic."

Apparently it's often burnt on fires to drive away the evil eye. Also, it's given orally to children, in small quantities, as a kind of general panacea.

I ask how much it costs. It works out at about £10 a kilo — three or four times as expensive as most of the herbs and potions around it. This seems to me to be a high price for something with only "bit of this, bit of that" applications. I'm dying to ask if it's eaten to induce visions, but it's a sensitive subject. Although the Berber affiliation to Islam is relatively casual, it's still a sin against reason to indulge in mind-altering drugs of any kind. And, if it's connected with local religious practices, it might not be considered discreet to talk about it to foreigners. Already, in the mountains, we've seen a number of whitewashed shrines to the local 'marabout,' or holy man; it took about a week before we found someone who was prepared to admit to us what they were.

I decide to ask him if the seeds are safe to eat, or if they're poisonous. He grins.

"No. You mustn't eat too many of them. Otherwise..." He spins his finger round his temple in the universal symbol for craziness.

I take a kilo.

☆ ☆

I pass a sample of the seeds over to Skip in London. He chews a couple up, invites me to do the same. They release a bitter juice which sets my teeth on edge. He tells me that's the harmaline: psychoactive plant alkaloids are almost always characterised by a bitter taste.

The seeds are the most potent part of the plant, with a concentration of harmaline from somewhere between 2 and 7%. Skip performs a fractional distillation, and estimates the active content at around 4 or 5%. He chews up the rest of the sample I gave him over a period of days — a tiny, almost homeopathic dose, but he reports dancing blue patterns on the point of sleep, and unusually lucid dreams.

About 5mg of harmaline constitutes an active dose. That's about a gramme of these seeds — provided we can find a method for extracting all the harmaline. If the extraction is partial, we'll need a little more. But, with a thousand grammes to play with, we should be able to get something going.

We decide to prepare the seeds along the lines described in the Avestas. First, pound them finely, using a pestle and mortar. Then mix them with milk, warming them slowly until the harmaline dissolves into it. In the Vedic version, of course, this mixture is then strained through a woollen cloth.

For an MAOI catalyst, we select ephedrine, for three reasons. First, it's the active alkaloid in ephedra, the combinant most often used in the Zoroastrian hom rites. Second, its own effect is that of a very mild stimulant, so it shouldn't interfere with the *harmal's* effect in the way that psilocybin might. Third, it's now quite freely available in England in the form of *khat,* the fresh plant stalks which are commonly chewed by Somali and Yemeni people. There's a plane which flies fresh supplies into London twice a week to service the local communities.

As for a location, we decide that, given the internal

nature of the experience, it's probably not necessary to struggle out to the back of beyond. In fact, it would be kind of useful to have a gas stove, cushions and other civilised amenities. We decide to go down to Leo's house in Devon, where tranquility and calm can be assured.

We arrive to find Claudia busy with her Brazilian umbanda rituals, purifying the house and asking for protection if our spirits should go a-wandering. Every alcove in the house is filled with tiny saucers of popcorn, coconut rum and dried seaweed from the beach, in honour of the sea mother Yemanja. Every corner is cleansed with a puff of cigar smoke.

We set to with pestle and mortar but the seeds prove almost impossible to grind: they're tough and resinous. We resort to pepper-mills; the obvious answer would be an electric coffee-grinder but we don't have one. Nor did the *yazna* priests, as Skip points out. Let's follow the recipe this time, maybe get fancy later.

The first batch of pulverised *harmal* is ready. We mix it with full fat milk, and begin to heat it gently. It turns brownish, thickening with the seed-pulp. We boil up the khat stalks into a golden, sweet-tasting tea.

We're concerned about two things. First, whether these two MAOIs are going to combine and kill us. Second, if the *harmal* works, what exactly we are going to see and where we are going to go. There's no guarantee it'll be pleasant. Skip tells us that induction into harmaline intoxication is often accompanied by strong feelings that you're about to die: in fact, the precursor to the astral journey can be the sensation of death itself.

Jo, who's also a nurse, produces a range of prescription medicines and lays them out on the table. She suggests we take a small amount of valium to allay anxiety. A small amount of baclofen as a muscle relaxant. And anti-nausea pills as and when necessary.

We pour the simmered brew into cups, and pass them around. For good measure, Skip performs a full Kabbalistic blessing in Hebrew. By this stage, I've never felt so psychically protected in my entire life.

The brew is bitter beyond belief. Globs of fat and *harmal* oil float in the greyish suspension. The husks of seed material are gritty and indigestible. The wool cloth of the Vedas suddenly makes plenty of sense.

After a few small cups of the mixture, my gorge rises at the idea of drinking any more, even washed down with the delicious ephedra tea. This isn't simply the taste: my system is rebelling at the harmaline. Suddenly, I can taste its bitterness not just in my throat, but in my blood. My pores are leaking it. I can smell it on my fingers. I feel saturated with it.

Jo closes her eyes and becomes still. Leo fights the nausea, loses, throws up. He takes an anti-nausea pill and stretches out on the sofa.

I feel fairly normal, but gradually become aware of subtle alterations in my perception. I seem to have drifted outside time. Moments stretch into minutes. Space, too, is slightly altered. Sometimes the view from my chair seems to dominate the room, shrinking it; sometimes the other people in the room seem so far away I feel I have to raise my voice to communicate. I feel slightly queasy, which is leading to a dissociation from my body, a slight anaesthetic numbness. I can't tell what position my arms and legs are in without looking.

At this stage it's still possible to ignore the effects. Probably, if given to someone unawares, they would hardly be aware of the strangeness of this phase. But concentrating on it enhances it. It gradually becomes harder to speak.

I close my eyes, and notice blue spots of light dancing on my eyelids. But there are no visions yet.

I've found out more about the Amazon *ayahuasca* rituals

since last time. Lying still during the *ayahuasca* trip is supposed to be a bad sign. Whenever non-Indians take the potion, they always vomit, and then end up on their backs with their eyes closed. In the Indian tradition, this usually signifies terrifying or nightmarish visions: or, at least, visions which are arrested at the first phase — the seething vines which I remember so clearly. But I'm looking for more this time. Several *ayahuasca* techniques involve the ayahuasceros making sudden noises around the subjects' heads, waving torches in front of their eyes, dragging them to their feet. Experienced subjects can walk, talk and sing under the influence.

I fight the tendency to relax, sitting up and opening my eyes. Skip is still in control of his reflexes, able to talk. Jo, who's an experienced trance and hypnotic subject, revives briefly. We begin to flip through books — a series of huge Victorian red leather-bound volumes on archaeology, in French, watercolour illustrations behind onion-skin paper. We fix on a series of plans of a Babylonian temple-complex, a ziggurat surrounded by a walled courtyard and surmounted by a copper-coated pyramid.

It gets dark, and we light candles. Immediately, the sensations become more intense. Glancing across the beam of a candle produces an intense flash of blue 'lightning' across the corner of the eye. We stare at one candle, closing our eyes, absorbing its flickering blue after-image through our eyelids. We read sections of the *Epic of Gilgamesh*. The words spool through my mind like a movie. I close my eyes, and see the walls of Uruk. (*"Are they not burnt brick and good?"*)

The temptation to lie down and close my eyes becomes stronger. I'd find it easier to fight if I knew exactly what the point of staying awake was. I close my eyes. Shadows begin to form around the after-images of the candle. I lie down.

As I do so, my body feels as if it's melted into the floor. It feels supremely comfortable, as if it's being laid to rest, enabling my mind to wander freely. As I close my eyes, I feel

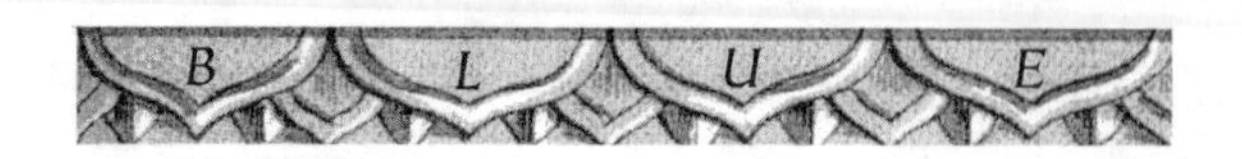

an abrupt tug inside my spinal cord, at the base of my brain. I feel as if something has disengaged. My vision no longer registers simple dots of light: I'm moving forwards through them, smoothly, with a shark-like motion. I make out walls on the periphery of my vision, as if I'm passing through a maze. They seem to be rough, as if made of mud, or carved out of rock. I'm passing through narrow streets, like the medina of a medieval Arab city. Figures pass me, dressed in robes and scarves. I try to take control of the vision, and retrace my steps. I move backwards, down the passage I've just emerged from. It's exactly the same as before. I drift forwards again. Ahead of me are dark figures, outlined in blue. They feel like giants. The blue light surrounding them seems to flow, like elctricity. One of them turns towards me, and stretches out a hand. The gesture impacts across my vision, like a blow to the forehead. Blue flashes burn across my eyes.

I open my eyes suddenly, to the dark, candle-lit room. I can't remember where I've just been. It feels like waking up, but I'm sure I haven't been asleep. Everyone else is silent. I get up to make a cup of tea. It's surprisingly easy to move. I feel entirely in control. It's almost as if nothing has happened: as if I just lay down, dozed and woke up.

This pattern continues for most of the night. We alternately lie down, wake up, sit and drink tea, discuss what's going on. Like the *ayahuasca,* we all share the jumping-off point of the visions: spots of blue light, the sensation of motion. Thereafter, we all seem to have been to different places. Jo has had the sensation of being shown a series of familiar plants and herbs, and lectured by an unseen voice about their medicinal and healing properties. I don't get a clear idea from anyone else. I'm probably pretty useless at describing my own.

I'm sure that the purpose of the rite is to ensure that everyone has the same vision. I'm sure it can be done. I still can't figure out how.

Eventually, physical mobility becomes harder.

Overwhelming tiredness takes over. I stumble upstairs to sleep, still moving relentlessly through strange landscapes every time I close my eyes. As my consciousness gives up its grip, I have a strong feeling that these visions are very like dreaming, but with a waking mind, with far more conscious control. I remember thinking that sleep gives us the world of dreams with one hand, and robs us of it with the other.

I'm trying to hang onto a particular landscape, which I'm witnessing with incredible clarity, when I wake up ten hours later. In the afternoon light, all the waking, sleeping, talking, reading, meditating and dreaming — which seemed so separate at the time — have merged into a continuum. Now, after a coffee and a cigarette, it feels as if I was taken, half-anaesthetised, on a journey to some other land I never knew existed.

4

TRANSCENDENTAL MEDICATION

Like the *ayahuasca* many years ago, my first *harmal* trip has left me with much to think about and many questions to answer. Unlike the *ayahuasca,* I have the material for further experiments: a large jar still full of seeds. I sacrifice a few to burning as an incense on charcoal, to get a feeling for their modern Iranian use. They smell nothing like they taste: aromatic, musky, with an astringent cleanness behind the perfume. Quite the most pleasant incense I've ever smelt. I fumigate my room with it and settle down to consider how to proceed.

First of all, I can now reassess the literature I've come across on harmaline. One of the reasons it seems to have been so little studied is that many accounts state that it's not really a psychedelic substance. This view seems to have been generated by people studying *ayahuasca* use, who point out quite correctly that much of the psychedelic effect of *ayahuasca* is due to the DMT. The inference from this is that the main reason for the presence of the harmaline-containing vine is simply to make the DMT orally active.

My experience of the *harmal* demonstrates that this isn't true, but also that it's understandable. *Harmal* certainly lacks many of the qualities associated with typical psychedelics, which produce a far more pervasive, relentless altering of reality over which the subject has little or no conscious control. Harmaline, by contrast, seems to work as much or as little as the subject requires. The immersion in its visual hallucinations is more palpable and 'real' than that of all but the strongest psychedelics; at the same time, though, it's possible to snap out of of them almost entirely, and just make a cup of tea or answer the phone.

If I had to compare its effects to something else, it wouldn't be another drug at all. It's like hypnosis in the sense that the subject appears to be physically poleaxed and off in another world, whereas the subjective effect is by contrast extremely light. It's like a sensory deprivation tank in the sense that the ego, the 'I' that sees, remains intact but almost entirely separate from the body, which seems to have been temporarily removed to another dimension. Most of all, perhaps, it's like dreaming: lucid dreaming, where the subject is awake in the dream and able to focus and manipulate the strange, other-worldly images which present themselves. The quality of the visions, too, is far closer to dreams than other psychedelic drugs. However strange the images which spring to mind under the influence of hallucinogens, it's usually plain, at least in retrospect, that their roots were in some scrambled sensory distortion of the world outside. The visions of *harmal,* like those of dreams, seem to come from another space altogether, one far removed from whatever external stimuli may have been present at the time.

Thinking back to my first experiment, I trust my initial instincts to attempt to simulate the pressing and drinking of *soma/haoma* and to concentrate on the manifestations of the *harmal* which fitted most closely with what I was looking for. Now, though, I'd like to run some controls. Change the means

of ingestion. Change the set and setting. Offer the seeds to other people without my interest in the mystery of *soma*, and listen to what they have to say about where the plant takes them. See how far the famed specificity of action of harmaline can produce the same experience in different people.

One thing I'd like to change is the nauseous quality of the brew. Warm, fatty milk isn't a favourite at the best of times; combined with the excruciating bitterness of the seeds, it's really quite an ordeal to hold down enough of the liquid to get the full effect.

I enlist Skip's help again, who suggests that I experiment with a little kitchen chemistry. Harmaline, harmine and the other harmala alkaloids or beta-carbolines aren't the only complex organic chemicals in the *harmal* plant. There are several others — the red dye which is extracted with vinegar and used to dye fezzes, for example. There's also a lot of cellulose and general plant material which probably isn't too tasty — *harmal,* after all, isn't exactly a delicacy. Most of this extraneous material can be reasonably simply extracted.

This may make the *harmal* easier to consume, but it's never going to be pleasant. Harmaline itself is an emetic, and has been used as such both in traditional and modern medicine. The same thing which is having the effect is still liable to make you throw up.

Nevertheless, we decide to have a go. Louise and I buy some isopropyl alcohol, borrow a friend's coffee-grinder and set to work.

First, we roast the seeds slowly in a pan. Above a certain temperature, the harmaline will break down, but a gentle application of heat evaporates some of the dyes and makes the seeds blister and spit like popcorn. Then we put the roasted seeds in the coffee-grinder and produce a reddish-brown powder. This looks like ground coffee and smells surprisingly delicious, roasted, nutty and slightly spicy. It looks as if it might smoke well with tobacco, so we try it. It burns rather hot,

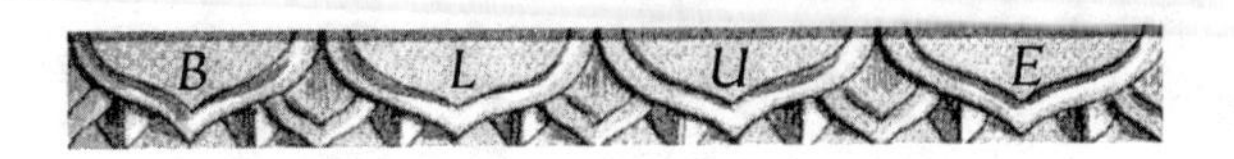

tending to congeal into little burning coals, but it tastes very pleasant, rather like the incense. It's a little rough on the throat, but the main problem with this method is that you'd have to smoke an unfeasibly large quantity of it to approach the 300mg or so which constitutes an active dose. We need to work further with an oral preparation.

We fill a coffee filter with roasted *harmal* grounds and drip isopropyl through it slowly. The liquid which emerges at the other end is a dark ruby red, an interesting echo of the Avestan description of *haoma*-juice as reddish-brown: clearly this method is bringing the red dye out with it too. We wait for the alcohol to evaporate and are left with a red, sticky oil. This presumably contains all the alcohol-soluble alkaloids in the plant and none of the inert plant material.

We christen this ruby oil 'red mercury'. It certainly has a higher concentration of harmaline than the seeds: probably approaching about fifty percent by weight. It can be smoked in a glass pipe, heating it gently from the outside so as not to break too much of the harmaline down. It can also be put into gel-caps and swallowed, making ingestion far easier. But the nausea and the effects remain largely inseparable. An active dose is always accompanied by the smell of harmaline on the skin, in the pores of the fingers, and the churning stomach which soon becomes numb, distant and is forgotten.

I make some enquiries on the internet while I'm engaged in this, offering my work-in-progress suggestions and casting around for anyone who can answer my questions. Eventually I'm referred to someone else who's engaged in similarly arcane practices. He's making a drink he calls 'rue brew' from Syrian Rue seeds, and is having an interesting time working with it. Eventually we speak on the phone. He's called Greg, he lives in

North London and he invites me to dinner.

I set out for the evening an hour or so before a partial eclipse of the sun. Up Ladbroke Grove, the rooves are crammed with people wearing shades and waving pinhole squares of cardboard. The effect is somehow apocalyptic, like an H.G.Wells fantasy about an approaching comet. It's high summer, and the sun beats down with a force which seems all the stronger for its unwonted human scrutiny.

I arrive at Greg's just as the eclipse is approaching. We sit out in the street to watch it. While everyone else is fiddling with smoked glass and mirrors, Greg has a better idea. He disappears into the house and reappears with a multi-faceted quartz crystal. Tilting it towards the sun, we see the eclipse reduplicated across the crystal's face in dozens of perfect miniatures.

Greg turns out to be a trader and marketer of natural Third World foodstuffs, responsible for bringing items like mung beans into the health food shops and subsequently into the supermarkets. He's very excited about *harmal,* reckons somebody should get in there now, start planting and buying futures. He thinks it has the potential to produce a natural, organic, mildly psychoactive coffee substitute with a huge global market.

We sample his 'rue brew,' which is basically the roasted, ground seeds drunk black with honey or sugar. It's not unpleasant, but the bitterness of the harmaline still seeps through the sweetening. He drank it on a daily basis for several weeks, and found that it produced a mild but pervasive dreaminess, unobtrusive in normal life but noticeable whenever he shut his eyes to dream or meditate. He found himself in a state where he could function perfectly normally, but whenever he chose to he could drift off on the blue tide of dreams. After a few weeks, though, he began to notice his urine becoming greenish-yellow, and stopped drinking it out of concern that its constant presence was impairing his kidney functions. He thinks this was probably do to with the presence of cheese, yoghurt and other tyramine-containing foods in his diet, which is of course a potential problem with any food or drink which is also an MAOI. But he too is fascinated by the *harmal* visions, and has continued using it on an irregular basis with no ill-effects.

☆ ☆

Another person who's been using it on a daily basis is Skip, who's waiting for a hip replacement operation and spending most of his time bed-ridden on various heavy pain medications. He gets into the habit of drinking a cup of it before going to bed, and spending his previously uncomfortable and semi-conscious nights floating off into its world of visions. He reports that, in several half-waking states, he's found himself returning to the same visionary worlds, corridors and cities peopled by entities whose presence he feels rather than sees. Many are pleasant, but some are not: he reports visiting one particular "Lovecraftian space" where he finds himself in partial sleep paralysis, moving involuntarily through icy blue caverns and corridors with people frozen into the walls, knowing that if he stops moving he'll freeze too. This space seems to be occupied by entities which he calls "the Daa," after the *'daa...daa'* sound which always seems to echo round the caverns.

I'm perennially interested in these accounts of 'entities' which present themselves regularly to people under the influence of certain drugs. Mushrooms, for example, are associated across many cultures with the presence of pixies or "little people," DMT, more recently, has generated repeated reports of contact with elvish "aliens." Clearly, this is one of the most concrete examples of the ways in which psychedelics seem to have the ability to take their subjects into a notional space which appears to exist in some sense objectively and independently. Clearly, too, this is the framework in which *soma* was experienced and in which, like the traditional use of *ayahuasca* today, it achieved its exalted status as the Elixir of the Gods.

But I've always been agnostic about how and in what sense these realms of transcendent identities 'exist' independently. My experiences with *harmal* have produced visions for which I can't begin to account, and which bear the impression of presences other than my own. But this usually seems to me to be a part of a constantly-shifting phantasmagoria, rather than a definite world to which I constantly return.

The clinical or psychological explanation of these entities is of course a description in terms of 'delusion' or 'hallucination,' which explains the transcendental realm away without answering any of the interesting questions about what leads to these perceptions, let alone what they might signify. There have been some attempts made to suggest why some minds might tend especially to construe these experiences in terms of independent entities, but these hypotheses — 'temporal lobe lability,' 'boundary deficit disorder' — are still little more than imaginative labels slapped over vast oceans of ignorance.

More interesting, if no more conclusive, are the various schemes and systems which have been presented as objective 'maps' of the levels of reality and hyper-reality to which psychedelic drugs open the door. The scientist John Lilly, model for the movie *Altered States,* presented perhaps the classic of this type of formulation thirty years ago, as a result of his intensive self-experimentation with psilocybin mushrooms and sensory deprivation tanks. Employing broadly scientific methodology, he characterised the human brain as a 'biocomputer' with various clearly-defined and 'programmable' levels of reality, and an army of 'spirit guides' and entities which existed to open the doors between them.

But, despite its poker-face of scientific objectivity, it's hard to ignore the similarities between Lilly's project and, for example, the plethora of kaballistic formulations of the various spheres of existence, or Rudolf Steiner's obsessively detailed hierarchies of elves, slyphs and sprites which in his scheme

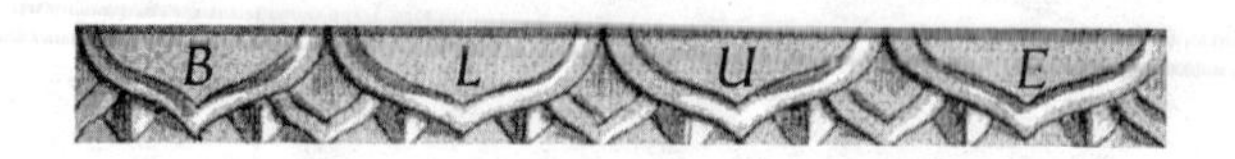

occupy the higher realms of existence. All of these systems may express complex truths in an elegant way, but the more they insist on their claim to sole and objective reality, the more irresistable it becomes to see in them the personal and idiosyncratic traits of their authors.

This question of whether there's a single transcendent reality 'out there' obviously bears heavily on any modern attempt to penetrate the ancient mysteries of *soma*. If we succeed in identifying the plant which it was, will it necessarily take us to the same Realm of the Gods? Or, if someone were — subjectively, of course — to enter the world of *soma*, would it follow that they'd found (objectively) the same plant? On the one hand, the chemical action of the plant in question must still be the same as it ever was. On the other, if the 'cultural matrix' of its use has vanished, does that mean that the experience has too?

Much of this paradox is wrapped up in the history of the search for *soma*. Thomas de Quincey, the man to whom Western fascination with Oriental drug use can most clearly be traced, also represents a watershed in the human view of the relationship between drug and mind which marks the modern territory. Before de Quincey, the view of drug-induced religous experience would have been something else entirely: typically, such experiences were simply part of the set of religious experience, the fact that they were produced by the agency of drugs being only a secondary detail. Since de Quincey, our separation of drugs from the culture which surrounded them, and our ever more spectacular ability to describe and control their chemical *modus operandi*, has made drug use a substantively different thing from what it was before. It's no longer possible to accept that drugs simply 'do' the same thing to everyone, now that we've eaten the apple of self-knowledge and appreciated all the ways in which the drug interacts with the mind and personality of the subject. Like some quantum experiment, the tools which we're now using to search for *soma*

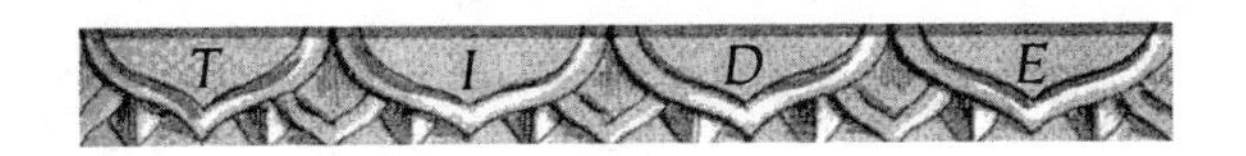

may, in the process, have altered our understanding of the thing we're looking at.

But even if this process has in itself made the recovery of the world of *soma* impossible, it's premature to declare this a tragedy until we've had a good look at the entirely new realms of drug experience which the same process has been opened up. The most obvious of these is perhaps our increasing ability to conceive an Other World in ways that are not religious at all. This, too dates back to the beginning of our modern story — most conspicuously, the pioneer of Oriental drug tourism, Moreau de Tours. Before Moreau, it would have been hard to imagine that the use of psychedelic drugs could be genuinely transcendental without being religious. But his invention of self-experiemental psychology was the first fully-fledged exploration of the further dimensions of the mind in a way which was specifically intended to undermine the assumption that these realms were in any way divine. Instead, his work suggests that it may be premature to assign the Other World to God — or to the legions of transcendental entities — until we've researched more thoroughly the possibility that it may be something newer and even stranger: a remote and otherwise inaccessible *terra incognita* within our own modern, individuated selves.

Moreau's legacy represents an entirely new way of viewing the interaction of drug and mind, and one which since his time has developed surprisingly little. Perhaps in response to the religious denigration of drug-induced wisdom, the high-profile champions of the drug experience from William James to Aldous Huxley have typically sought to defend it by claiming that the world reached through drugs is just as spiritually valid as that reached through other religious means — rather than asking why drug experiences should need to validate themselves in religious terms at all.

And yet it takes a hard-nosed rationalist indeed to view the Other World opened up by psychedelic drugs as purely the domain of science. It remains a process of initiation which resolutely continues to resound with the echoes of hidden wisdom and rites of passage which characterise its ancient and traditional use. By the same token, also, the ancient and traditional use of drugs itself resonates at least in part with the precepts of science: the systematic process of understanding and harnessing the natural world. Perhaps it's unreasonable to expect the experiences which drugs offer to be either 'purely' scientific or 'purely' magical, since it's arguable that they've never been either one or the other.

One of the effects of this ambiguity has been that, at the same time as our scientific understanding of drugs has progressed immeasurably, the drug counterculture which has evolved alongside it is perhaps the clearest example of a global initiatory secret society to have sprung from the elective, pluralist dynamics of modern capitalism. To join it is to learn the whispered lore of picking mushrooms and cultivating cannabis, to enter a clandestine world of esoteric knowledge and covert supply through the traditional initiatic routes of oral transmission, songs and dances, secretly-circulated texts.

But this isn't the world of *soma*: *soma* is the expression of a world where humanity is united in its ability to reach the Other World, where drug use is universally valued as the key to divine experience. To explore today's drug experience is, by contrast, to remove oneself from consensus reality and enter the world of the forbidden. In this sense, modern drug use is far closer to the other persistent Oriental drug myth, that of the Assassins. The Old Man and his cohorts sprang not from a Golden Age where all humanity formed a group mind, but from a world in which they were marginalised, criminalised and demonised. Their strategy was to develop an initiatory counterculture which took them even further outside society, in the same way in which the mysteries of temporary ego-death and the Other World which lies beyond it take the modern drug user far outside the world of legitimised consumer choice and offer them an experience which 'normal life' emphatically doesn't.

The illegal status of drug use undoubtedly contributes to its secret initiatory qualities, but at the root of these is not merely the law but the nature of the experience itself. For the Club des Hachichins, for example, drug use was entirely legal, but they recognised nevertheless that the jewelled realms of intoxication which they visited should be protected from the profane world by ritual and secrecy.

With all this in mind, I recognise that any attempt to enter the imaginal world of the original *soma* is, at best, a guerilla raid. But, by the same token, such an attempt also has the possibility of opening up something entirely new, a dimension of mind which is perhaps only just coming into being.

Thanks to the pioneering efforts of Greg and Skip, a pattern is beginning to form around the effects of constant, low-level doses of *harmal*. But the other question which interests me is the effect of a high-level dose, two or three times more than I've been taking. I haven't done this, partly because the effects would undoubtedly include high levels of nausea, but also because I'm unaware of the ceiling of physical safety. With most traditional psychedelics, toxic doses are many orders of magnitude greater than effective doses, and a high dose produces nothing more than a more intense mental bombardment; with harmaline, between three and five times the effective dose produces significant levels of toxicity.

Fortunately someone else does this experiment for me. I gave a bag of seeds to Charlie before he moved to Australia; a few weeks later, I receive his account by email:

We took a trip up the coast a few hours drive to this beautiful lake/lagoon spot where we camped. Gorgeous sunsets and creature/bird noises. Mark saw a kangaroo and so was a happy man. We brewed up a big batch of Harmaline in some milk Milo. We'd ground up about half a packet of seeds before we went. Some very gung-ho sub-personality must have taken me over, as I directed Shelley to bung it all in the brew (even though I had no idea of sensible doses). It was truly disgusting – as you know – bitter and gritty. Mark and I had full cups and Shell had very little, her stomach flatly refusing to ingest such stuff in quantity. Then a little later half a teaspoon of 'shrooms to catalyse. Nothing much happened, and then the tell-tale flashing things at the edge of the field of vision started happening. The stars were intense (in reality) and it was as though there were shooting stars everywhere. Physical coordination started to go very haywire – like drunk, only more disorienting and made worse by movement, so we started to subside. I gamely went for half a cup more brew, which was rash because we were still on the way up.

Nausea started to get pretty intense and I had a long phase of vomiting and felt pretty lousy. Stumbling about vomiting and complaining. Shelley said I was quite impossible. Looked into the car boot for something and *Oh my God* – weird visual light-show. Streamers of light everywhere, flashing and zipping across the visual field.

But standing up and moving about was becoming awful so we gradually collapsed into lying-down-mode.

I was really rather panicked. I don't know why but I didn't make the connection that this was a plant hallucinogen, and that therefore some unwanted physical effects were probably par for the course. I just remember thinking – shit what if I've really had loads too much.

Then started what I believe is one of the most characteristic effects of *harmal*. Mark and I both noticed it. Not hallucinations but the ability to be able to conjure up amazing visual scenes in the minds eye – in full detail and 24-bit colour. You thought of it, and it was there, and you could examine it or go into it or embroider it with no effort at all. I think *Harmal* is an imagination-enhancer, rather than a true hallucinogen.

I also imagined a lot of things (eyes open) and then

they turned out to be something else entirely. I guess this is kind of hallucinogenic.

Another effect was some amazing flashbacks. Links between things became obvious. I remember recalling with astonishing clarity something you said to me Mike (I forget what now) but it seemed very important at the time and very wise too.

Of course this went on and on and on. We had no idea how much we had taken compared to a notional recommended dose, but a lot and I kind of wondered when it would stop.

I guess this was after about 6 hours and things had quietened down a mite, but I was still nauseous, stumbling and totally off on one. I remember thinking that it might go on the next day. And so at 3am to bed. And kind of a trance, rather than sleep. Immobile, semiconscious, mind and imagination wandering.

Of course by 11am things were back to normal again. But quite a roller-coaster.

☆ ☆

Even allowing for the small handful of mushrooms, this demonstrates that harmaline does indeed have a powerful psychedelic action. I was to reach this kind of effect eventually, though without a noticeable increase in dose.

So my first major doubt about the identification of *harmal* as *soma* — that it's not psychoactive without other tryptamines — is answered to my satisfaction. The second objection is that it's not used as a hallucinogen in the indigenous cultures where it grows. This is hard to answer so directly, but I decide to investigate it. An archaeologist friend recommends that I talk to a Professor Gordon Hillman at the Institute of Archaeology in London, who he tells me is the world expert on the botany, ancient and modern, of the Middle East.

Gordon Hillman is delighted that someone is researching *Peganum Harmala*. He waxes enthusiastic about it: what a beautiful plant, what wonderful flowers, how he once came across an entire field of it growing in a *wadi* in central Syria, with a tribe of Bedouins camping right beside it. He's been studying it quite intensively, on and off, for at least twenty years. He's so enthusiastic that I assume he must know what it is that I'm interested in. I ask him if he knows anything about its, ah, ritual uses.

Yes, indeed. The seeds are burnt quite commonly as an incense in Iran. If you dissolve the seeds and sal ammoniac in brandy for six months, you can produce a red dye which used to be used to produce fezzes in Anatolia.

I prod him a little further, trying to choose my words so as not to sound like a crazed drug addict. I mean, its ritual use in terms of...ingesting it to produce trance states and visions.

He's astonished. Good Lord! You mean it's... hallucinogenic?

I'm astonished too. How come he's been studying it for twenty years and never noticed?

He explains that *Peganum Harmala* grows typically on over-grazed steppe: high, dry mountain plateau, stripped of vegetation and fertilised by sheep and goats. In antiquity, its habitat included parts of Syria, Anatolia, Egypt, Iran and Central Asia. As overcultivation extended out of the former fertile crescent, so *harmal* spread to Greece, Italy, North Africa and Eastern Europe, where you now find it as far north as Budapest. As such, the spread of the plant is a valuable index to the growth of agriculture through history.

In turn, he asks me what I've found out about it. I tell him about *soma, haoma* and the Zoroastrians. I tell him about *ayahuasca* and the Amazon. I tell him about harmaline. His jaw drops open. This is all news to him.

I explain that my main interest in all this is to try and locate a culture which may still be using *harmal* in a ritual manner. His eyes light up. In the light of what I've just told him, a number of things are starting to make sense.

He remembers travelling in the Konya plain, in central Turkey, and coming across a huge field of *harmal*. In the middle of this field was a tree, which he wandered over to examine. As he approached it, he made out splashes of blood on the ground beneath it: some dried black, some fresh. Looking up into the tree, he saw its branches festooned with goats' feet and chickens' heads, tied with string like Christmas decorations. A totem tree.

The local inhabitants were a tribe of formerly nomadic Turkamans known as the Kizikbas, or 'red-headed'. He made his way towards their nearest village to make some more enquiries. On the way, he met an old Kizilbas working in the field. He gestured back at the tree, its solitary outline rising out of the plain of *harmal*.

"Could you tell me about that tree?," he asked. "What tree?," replied the Kizilbas, and walked off. Professor Hillman decided, on second thoughts, not to visit the village.

Later, I find out a little more about the Kizilbas. Their 'red-headed' epithet refers to their traditional red headgear; beyond this, there seems to be a level of vagueness about who exactly they are. Some people seem to define them broadly as a range of Shiite sects including the Alevis, who formerly extended into Syria and Persia and were closely connected with the Nizari Ismai'lis: the Assassins, no less.

More strictly, the term seems to refer to an ethnic Turcoman people whose red headgear marks their alleigance to an obscure religious sect of Shiite leanings. It seems that, during the sixteenth century, they came under the threat of religious persecution and allied themselves with the powerful order of Bektashi sufis or 'dervishes'. The Bektashis' most holy city was (and is) Konya, the birthplace of the great sufi poet Rumi, and it was here that Gordon Hillman found his totem tree.

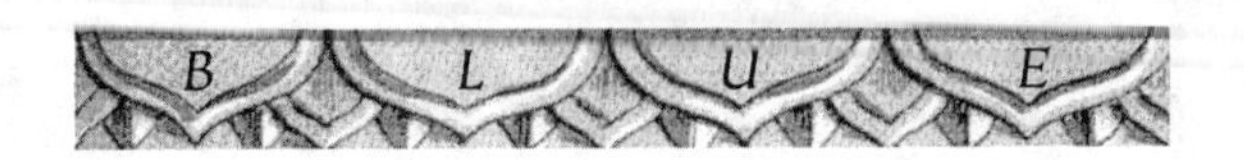

This connection with the sufi orders of Konya makes it highly likely that the Kizilbas tradition might, at least in the past, have encompassed the use of power plants: the Bektashi poetry speaks eloquently and frequently of hashish and opium as paths to the divine. Gordon Hillman's encounter suggests that these paths may have included *harmal*, too.

This also starts me speculating about the Kizilbas and the 'fez red' dye which is, of course, also extracted from *harmal* seeds. It could be that the Kizilbas simply use the plant for dyeing their trademark red headgear. But it could be the other way around: that the significance of the red fez across the Near East was originally connected in some way with the plant's other properties.

In this case, the effective suppression of these traditions may have tken place not with the arrival of Islam, but as recently as the beginning of this century. Under the Ottomans, the Turkish sufi orders were highly respected and the traditional fez worn by almost every male. It was only after the First World War that Kemal Ataturk, in his drive to modernise the crumbling Turkish empire, suppressed the sufi and dervish orders like the Bektashis — and, specifically, prohibited the wearing of the fez.

Gordon Hillman remembers something else, too: a few years ago, when he was visiting Harvard Botanical Museum, he was introduced to an extremely old lady, in at least her mid-eighties, who was writing a paper on *Peganum Harmala*. He can't remember her name, or the subject-matter, but he's sure it was to do with ritual use. He has a feeling it was concentrating on early travellers' chronicles from the nineteenth century.

I make some enquiries at Harvard Botanical and locate the old lady. Her name is Dorothy Kamen-Kaye. She's apparently in her mid-nineties, rarely visits the campus, and has a hearing problem which means she doesn't use the phone. I fire off a hopeful air-mail letter, explaining that what I'm interested in is probably peripheral to her studies — and, of course, being careful to use words like 'trance' and 'visionary' rather than 'drug' and 'psychedelic.'

I needn't have bothered. A week or two later I get an air-mail letter covered in excited, spidery handwriting. *"Your research is not peripheral to my work...I'm glad you wrote! The whole P. Harmala business has been jinxed; perhaps you & I together can salvage something..."*

It turns out that she's been studying the journals of a Victorian traveller called William Gifford Palgrave, brother of the compiler of the famous poetry anthology *Palgrave's Golden Treasury*. Palgrave, something of a Munchhausen character who was obviously aware of the credulity and hunger for the exotic among the Victorians, claimed to have made all manner of valuable scientific discoveries which were tragically 'lost' in a shipwreck of which no-one else seems to have any record. But one of his tales intrigued Dorothy especially: the use of a strange "narcotic plant" in Syria, whose seeds were added to coffee and produced a hallucinogenic effect. (Unfortunately, his sample of the seeds also 'disappeared' in the shipwreck.)

Dorothy, a folklorist and botanist, was particularly interested by this description which, while not necessarily reliable, seemed nevertheless to describe something which was neither cannabis (the seeds of which are inactive) nor opium (which isn't a hallucinogenic stimulant). She started going through various eighteenth- and nineteenth-century botanical works looking for an alternative.

And she found *harmal*.

After reading so often that there's no record of *harmal* being employed as a psychedelic since its notional use in ancient times, I'm astonished by what Dorothy has turned up. No less than the father of modern botany, Linnaeus, described it in the first-ever compendium of psychedelic plants, his *Inebrianta*, published in 1762:

"Peganum Harmala, whose seeds the Turks have for sale in their markets, is an inebriant, according to Belon in his travel account, who relates (with Giovio as his witness) that the emperor Soliman used to eat this seed not knowing its nature, because it brought pleasure and took away the memory of troublesome affairs."

Through the nineteenth century, similar reports continue from Turkey, Morocco and across the Near East. We read of the seeds of *harmel* or *al-harma* producing a *"delicious intoxication,"* a *"state of mirthful euphoria and great joy."* Far from being forgotten in antiquity, *harmal* intoxication seems indeed to have continued unremarked under the cloak of Islam.

I continue corresponding with Dorothy, and send her some *harmal* seeds. She's delighted that someone else is looking into an area which has been a private interest for so long. As we swap letters, more and more remarkable sections of her life story emerge. She spent much of the 1940s and 1950s in Venezuela and Central America. She was the first Westerner to write about the Trinidad steel drums. Many of her folkloric and ethnographic papers describe practices previously unknown to science, and most of them have never been followed up. Our exchanges spread to encompass an eclectic range of shared interests — hashish-growing in Morocco, treasure-hunts in Caribbean wrecks, British bonfire night traditions, Henry de Montfried's books about smuggling in the Red Sea — and continue to this day.

☆ ☆

I join an internet discussion group for people interested in Iranian culture, and perform a quick survey of *harmal, esfand* and the current state of knowledge about its use. Everyone seems to be familiar with it: the dried seeds are sold in every spice-stall in the country. But the uses of it mostly reiterate what I've already heard. The seeds tend to be burnt on festive occasions, or to keep away the evil eye. They'll be burnt when you move into a new house, to keep away the jealously of spiteful neighbours, or to purify a room after someone you suspect of having evil intentions has been in it. Beggar women in the street will burn it, waft it under the noses of passers-by and demand money for the 'blessing,' much as European gypsies use sprigs of lavender wrapped in tinfoil.

But no-one seems to have heard of eating the seeds, or to be aware of any tradition of doing so.

One Iranian, living in London, points out to me that it's possible to buy *esfand* in Iranian food stores.

I find this hard to believe, but my hard-sought Moroccan kilo is dwindling fast. I wander down to a local Iranian store, and search among the pistachios, incenses, dried fruit and nuts. One bag of incense seems to have some *harmal* seeds in, mixed up with small chunks of resinous frankincense and perfumed dried flowers.

And, beside it, is a small bag filled entirely with *harmal* seeds, neatly sealed, enough for about ten doses.

It costs £1.75.

☆ ☆

I continue drinking *harmal* once every couple of weeks, setting an evening aside to try different mixtures, different preparations, different stimuli. Candle-light. Darkness. Music. But the visions remain frustratingly erratic. Once or twice, I notice no greater effect than a pleasant languor and colourful dreams. Often I find, after a few hours, I sink into a dramatically powerful vision where I lose my sense of self entirely, the spell of which is usually broken by the distinctive sharp tug at the base of the skull which leaves me sitting bolt upright, stone cold sober. I find that, once a vision like this has been interrupted, the trip is effectively over: the intensity of the

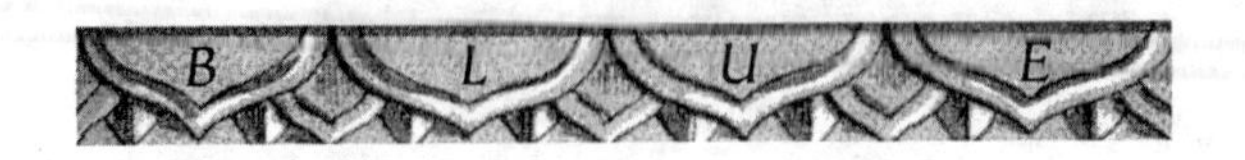

visions, once it's peaked, seems not to return.

Gradually, I begin to take the *harmal* at night, where the darkness intensifies the effect. I build up a collection of ancient epics and sufi poetry, which I read for hours on end.

On one occasion, this method is dramatically successful.

I set up a session with Boz, a native Iranian speaker who reads the entire *Hom Yasht* from the *Avestas* in the original old Persian. It sounds beautiful, but leaves me none the wiser — at least, as far as I can tell.

I then reach for another old Persian text, this time in translation: the *Arda Wiraz Namaq,* a visionary tract written many centuries later during the Sassanian period, after Alexander the Great (*"that wretched, wicked, heretic, sinful, maleficent Alexander the Roman"*) had wreaked his havoc across the Persian empire. It's the story of an especially righteous Zoroastrian, Wiraz, who is selected to undergo the ordeal of the original *haoma* and journey to the land of the gods for advice and guidance.

The question raised by this text is whether the secret of the original, hallucinogenic *haoma* was indeed preserved by the Zoroastrian priesthood up to this late date. On the one hand, there's no doubt that the *haoma*-pressing ritual survived in some form: we have seals from the treasury of Persepolis which show priests working with pestles and mortars around a thousand years after the introduction of the Hom Yasht. On the other hand, the plant extract which Wiraz takes isn't actually referred to as *haoma* — the word used is *mang,* a generic term meaning 'medicine' or 'drug'. Flattery and Schwartz point out that the *mang* in Wiraz's cup is described as *"mang of Wishtarp,"* which was an old epithet for *haoma*. Others point out that *mang* is cognate with *bhang,* and suggests a cannabis preparation. Still others regard Wiraz's drink as a metaphor for channelling the spirit of the ancient roots of Zoroastrianism.

Whatever, the description of Wiraz's ordeal does sound remarkably like *harmal* intoxication. He drinks three cups of the plant extract in milk, lies down and sleeps for seven days and

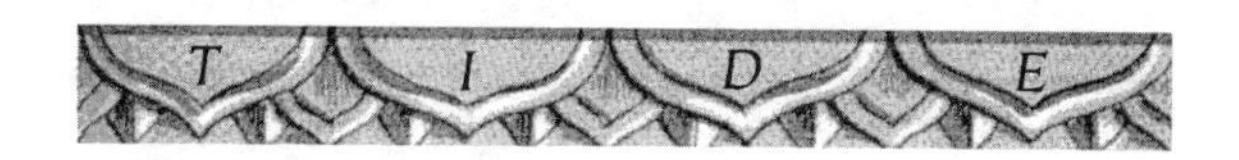

nights. When he awakes, he tells the story of his travels. The *mang* transported him into the realm of the gods, where he met with two guides who took him over a precarious bridge into the world of the afterlife: a classic shamanic encounter. Then one of the guides showed him the Paradise of the Righteous, the other the Inferno of the Wicked.

This heaven and hell clearly comes not from the original *haoma* experience of the ancient Magi, but from the dualist cosmos of Zoroaster, with its struggle between Ohrmazd and Ahriman, the principles of light and darkness. It occurs to me that the *Arda Wiraz Namaq* is two types of religious text rolled into one. First, it's a remembrance of the original spiritual journey of the *haoma* rite, which has been all but forgotten. Second, it's a fundamentalist text designed to reinforce the faithful in their return to the old ways. Shamanic travelling and fire-and-brimstone moralising sit side by side.

The Paradise of the Zoroastrians is very brief in comparison with the Inferno of the Wicked. This occupies most of the book, and conjures up images which make the wildest Christian hellfire rhetoric look insipid:

"...And I saw the souls of the women into both of whose eyes they had driven wooden pegs, hanging downwards by one leg. And many frogs, scorpions, snakes and other reptiles went into and came out of their mouths and noses and ears and anuses and vulvas. And from them had grown something like a hedgehog of iron with thorns, and the semen of all kinds of demons and the stench and the filth were going into their mouths and noses to a finger's depth. And I asked: 'Whose souls are these who are suffering such severe punishment?' Sros, the pious, and the god Adur, said: 'These are the souls of those wicked women who in the world were unfaithful to their husbands...' "

I look up from the photocopied pages, and twitch instinctively as an electric blue fireball flies past my face.

Simply the act or focusing on black-and-white text seems to have triggered an astonishing reaction. Before my waking eyes, blue bolts of light whizz and flash, so brightly I'm almost blinded. Boz and Paul wake up from their trances, where they've been listening to me read, and notice the same thing. For the first time in my *harmal* experiments, it's hardly possible any more to distinguish between what's real and what isn't. Closing my eyes, I'm sucked into a tunnel of light. Worlds are unfolding before me. I stumble to my feet, feel violently sick, stagger to the kitchen and throw up.

I feel much better. Generally speaking, I have a strong stomach: I've probably only vomited a handful of times in my adult life. I'd always had a rule of thumb that it wouldn't be worth taking any drug which would make you throw up. But this is different: it's effortless, without much of the discomfort that I normally associate with being sick.

I collapse back down again, and close my eyes. The familiar physical numbness is back, and my mind is rapidly receding into another space where my body seems far away. Images, crystalline in clarity, present themselves to me. I see a parade of men tramping through an ancient walled city, leading tethered birds shaped like geese, but the size of elephants. I see a point of light and surge towards it. I find myself breaking out of the top of an extinct volcano, and flying over a barren desert plateau, huge enough to make out the earth's curvature at the horizon.

I wake long enough to establish that Paul and Boz are OK. Both mutter blissful contentment, and close their eyes again. I decide to stagger to bed. Fighting my way through the blobs and flashes of light which crawl and hum across my waking vision, I collapse in the darkened bedroom.

An indeterminate length of time passes, visions streaming endlessly through my mind's eye. Suddenly, I'm aware of an outside sound — my bedroom door creaking open. My presence is required for some reason. I open my eyes to the noisy blackness, and stare towards the door.

A figure pushes through the door and stands in the

doorway. I blink and focus. It's wearing a crimson djellebah robe, with the hood up. I own such a djellebah. This must be Boz or Paul, wearing it for some reason.

I remember that the djellebah is in a drawer by my bedside.

I stare again at the figure. Behind it, the darkness swirls and boils like mercury. My eyes are drawn to its shadow. My gaze rushes through into the darkness, as if into a hall of infinite mirrors.

I baulk at this sudden motion, and try to refocus my gaze. I need to know who this is who is standing in front of me.

I pull back and refocus my eyes. The figure has vanished.

I remember reading the account of an Amazon *ayahuasca*-drinker who said that the visions he experienced with the brew were so beautiful that he used to put his hands over his eyes for fear that someone might try to steal them. I feel like doing the same.

☆ ☆

I'm interested to find out more about the actual mechanism of harmaline's action in the brain. It's so different in kind from any other drug that I wonder what part of the brain it's activating, and how much we know neurologically about where these visions might be coming from.

This proves to be another question which is more easily asked than answered. The mechanism of action of most psychedelic drugs is only partially understood: in fact, research into these drugs has opened up areas of exploration which were previously unknown. Far from tapping into a body of scientific knowledge which already exists, drug-induced altered states of consciousness have repeatedly, over the last fifty years, opened up neurological vistas previously undreamed of.

Basically, within the low-level field of electrical conductivity which is the medium of brain activity, messages are carried around the brain by chemical agents known as neurotransmitters, of which the best-known are probably dopamine and serotonin. Like sub-atomic particles, the number of neurotransmitters we know about has increased from a small handful to an ever-growing mass, often as a result of studying drug action. Trying to understand the action of PCP ("angel dust") led scientists to the discovery of glutamate, a basic neurotransmitter of the reticular system. More recently, in 1994, the mechanism of action of cannabis was finally understood: it's a natural analogue of a neurotransmitter which exists in the brain, an 'endo-cannabis' in the same way as endorphins ("endo-morphines") are our natural internal opiates. So cannabis and opiates work by flooding the brain with chemicals which are themselves designed to send out waves of signals, initiating 'cascade reactions' of other chemicals which translate these brain signals into powerful physical reactions.

In the early 1950s, it was discovered that when the neurotransmitter serotonin was incubated *in vitro* in the pineal gland tissue of mammals, it broke down into a range of complex organic metabolites. Serotonin itself is a tryptamine, and some of these metabolites were other methylated tryptamines, such as dimethoxy tryptamine — DMT. What's more, these in turn broke down into beta-carbolines — harmaline, tetra-hydro-harmine and the rest.

Various mammalian and human pineal glands were then analysed for these chemicals, and found to contain them. The extraordinary fact was that the *ayahuasca* brew of harmaline and DMT was actually present in the human brain.

Once this fact was discovered, the next question was what to do with it. To start with, it answered the basic question about how *ayahuasca,* DMT and harmaline work: our brains have receptor sites which are specifically designed for them. But the next question was what function they perform in their natural versions; or, to put it another way, what's the brain function of which these drugs give us an amplified form?

At this time, the mainstream model of psychedelic drug effects was known as "psychotomimesis": the idea that these chemicals were signifiers and producers of various states of mental illness and psychosis, and their effect was to mimic these states temporarily in the human brain. This, effectvely, was the model first suggested by Moreau de Tours in the 1840s. Along these lines, the neurologists Osmond and Smythies christened the endo-*ayahuasca* complex "endogenous schizotoxins," and pronounced their effects to be characteristic of hallucinatory psychoses.

The trouble with this was that these endogenous psychedelics are present not just in psychotics but in everyone, making them useless as a marker for psychosis: no difference was ever found in their levels between 'normal' and 'abnormal' brains. At the same time, the 'psychotomimetic' model was losing to ground to the 'psychedelic' model of drug action which claimed that these altered states of consciousness weren't necessarily shadows of mental illness, but represented brain-states quite different from either 'normal' or 'abnormal' minds. Since there were no obvious medical breakthroughs being offered by the "endogenous schizotoxins," the presence of harmaline and DMT in the brain became a mere curiosity.

The next piece of serious work on the psychological effects of harmaline came from an altogether different quarter. In the mid-sixties Claudio Naranjo, a Chilean psychoanalyst with gestalt-Jungian leanings, was working at the Esalen Centre, a mecca for New Age psychoanalysis in Big Sur, California, when he decided to visit the Amazon, giving as his reason that he *"wanted to go where people ate people."* He took with him some blotters of LSD, which he gave to some of the Indians he met. Impressed by his powerful medicine, they offered him theirs: *ayahuasca*.

Naranjo returned to civilisation with a consuming interest in using psychedelic drugs in psychoanalysis. He

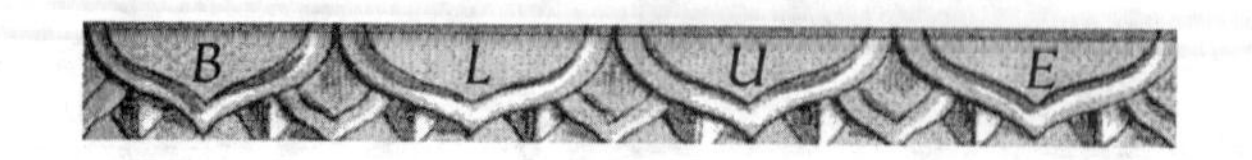

returned to Santiago in Chile, where drug restrictions were less tight, and spent 1965 and 1966 experimenting on patients with four different drugs: MDA, MDMA, ibogaine and harmaline.

He tried harmaline on around thirty subjects, some sixty per cent of whom were suffering from one form or another of neurotic disorder. He administered it in its pure laboratory form, in intravenous doses of 70 to 100 milligrammes. He noted none of the classic physical markers of the major psychedelics — no pupil dilation, no rise in blood pressure — but a pronounced stimulation of visual, eidetic imagery. He records the main effects as physical relaxation, a tendency to withdraw from the outside world of physical stimuli and to close the eyes, a physical numbness, and very vivid visual imagery ordered in meaningful dreamlike sequences. His recommended setting was a comfortable couch in a quiet, dark environment.

I'd go along with that.

The great advantage which he found harmaline offered to psychotherapy was the ability of the subject to control their visions. The major psychedelics — mescaline, LSD — tended to remove the patient's ability to control the intense flow of sensation and emotion, making them feel powerless and brittle, and often exacerbating syndromes of anxiety and low self-esteem. Harmaline, by contrast, allowed them to take control of the scenario which was being replayed in front of them, and use techniques of positive visualisation to direct and model the outcome in the direction of their ongoing therapy.

But it had disadvantages too. Guidance of the sessions was often very difficult, as the subject found all outside stimuli, including the analyst's voice, a distraction. Patients would often just mumble or grunt, obviously not wanting to talk. Intervention by the therapist was very hard to judge: the best results came when the subject was talking freely of their own volition, the therapist simply listening. When this didn't happen, many of the sessions were wasted. Intrusive surveillance, like wiring the subjects for EEG, often led to

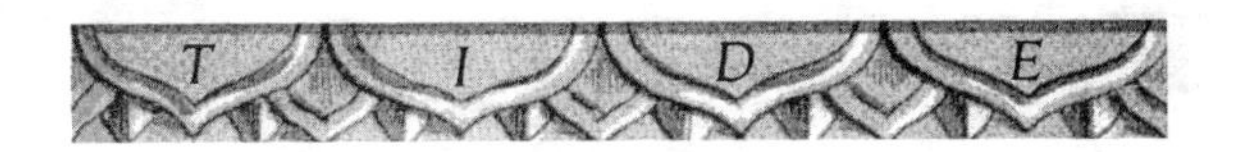

unpleasant, unproductive sessions.

The other problem with harmaline was that it was emotionally uninvolving. Unlike the hallucinogenic stimulants, which could be used to bring the subjects into the 'now' of past moments of defining crisis, the patients under harmaline remained detatched observers, recording their visual imagery almost objectively, as if they were watching a movie.

Naranjo was quick to notice the connections between the therapeutic content of the harmaline visions and the types of imagery which are associated with initiation in many indigenous cultures. Harmaline, he felt, plunges the mind into an area of myth which is the essence of initiation: an exposure to the symbols, stories and mysteries of adulthood in a form in which they can be experienced subjectively, but in a controlled set and setting.

But what particularly interested Naranjo was the similarity and content of all the subjects' visions. He began to record the most common visions — tigers and big cats, flying birds, dark-skinned men, images of death and abstract patterns revolving around a centre, source or axis. Comparing these to the *ayahuasca* literature, he found little difference between his subjects and the Indians. This led him to develop the idea that harmaline delivers access to the collective unconscious, a pool of mythic and archetypal imagery which exists independently of the individual.

It's this specificity of visions which interests me, but I still don't find the 'collective unconscious' theory entirely satisfying. First of all, I've now tried *harmal* many times, and so have many other people I know. Some of Naranjo's archetypes ring a bell — birds, flying, seeing landscapes from an aerial 'bird's eye view,' for example. But many of them don't: big jungle cats and dark-skinned men haven't occurred to me or anyone I've asked. To the extent that we've been 'programming' our trips with the imagery of the ancient Near East, I've noticed a strong body of imagery — mud-walled

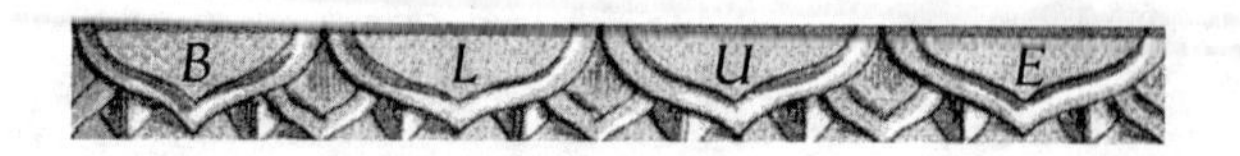

cities, deserts, arabesque gardens — which seem to occupy the same position as Naranjo's jungle imagery. (I wonder if he told his subjects that the drug was derived from a jungle power-plant?) I'm reluctant to accept a bedrock of mythic archetypes which seems so clearly to reflect the subject's self-programming: it strikes me as yet another 'true and objective map' of the protean, shifting world of brain-states, entities and higher realms of consciousness.

My feelings are somewhat supported by some research carried out during the 1970s on *ayahuasca*-using Indians by an anthropologist named Reichel-Dolmatoff, who gave his subjects a set of crayons and asked them to draw their *ayahuasca* visions. They apparently enjoyed this project, selecting almost exclusively the blue, red and yellow crayons and commenting that they would have appreciated a much wider range of colours in these areas. Their work revealed a strong similarity in the 'first stages' of hallucination — the geometric patterning — where they produced a very similar range of zigzags, circles and U-shapes, very much what I remember from my first *ayahuasca* trip in Wales. But the 'second stage,' the symbolic imagery which follows, displayed a far greater level of personal and cultural variation — suggesting that the only level on which the human response to *ayahuasca* is truly 'hard-wired' is in the geometrical 'entoptic' level of perception and mental processing.

Naranjo also uses the world of Jungian archetypes to explain different physical reactions to harmaline. Some subjects, he noted, were largely unsusceptible to the psychedelic effects of harmaline, having very little in the way of visions and experiencing only "malaise, somnolence and vomiting." His feeling is that this happens to individuals who are less comfortable with the archetypal "animal level of existence" to which harmaline takes them, and the nausea and vomiting are an autonomic reaction produced by the resisting mind.

There may be something to this, but it doesn't correlate entirely with my experience. After all, the only time I vomited

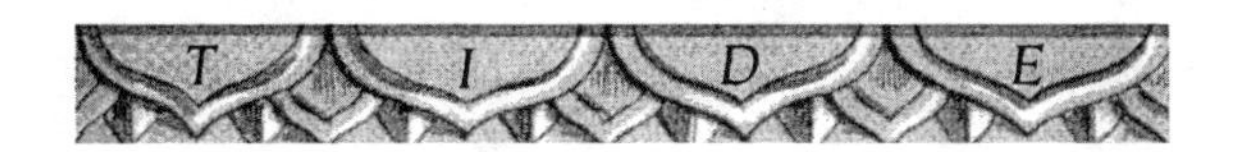

was also the time when I had my most powerful visions: physically, it felt not limiting but liberating. Vomiting may be a subconscious autonomic response; it may also be a physical reaction to a drug which is specifically used as an emetic. If I wanted to separate out a group of subjects into those who were likely to vomit and those who weren't, I wouldn't try Jungian analysis on them: I'd simply starve half of them for twenty-four hours and feed the others deep-pan pizzas.

But, by and large, Naranjo's experiment was a success. Out of his thirty subjects, he reckoned that around fifteen experienced some therapeutic benefit, and ten showed dramatic improvements comparable to a much longer period of intensive psychotherapy. He recommended overcoming the 'withdrawn' aspects of harmaline by combining it with MDA, a short-acting empathic stimulant which adds energy and interpersonal dynamics to the experience, as well as extending the effect to about twelve hours. He did, however, note an occasional abreaction with this combination: twice in about thirty sessions, the subject became confused, excited and physically out of control, thrashing around while talking to 'dream-companions.'

I note this for future reference.

Naranjo's harmaline work still stands as the most detailed investigation of the psychological effects of harmaline, but the neurological underpinning of the drug's action remain largely mysterious. Much of this mystery is connected with the organ of the brain in which harmaline and the other beta-carbolines naturally occur: the pineal gland.

The pineal gland, or epiphysis, is probably the most obscure and mysterious organ in the human brain, and is another prime example of such understanding as there is being led by drug research. Far from tapping into a solid body of orthodox neuroscience, the pineal gland presents us with a nest of suppositions and imponderables in which much of the dim light seems to be shed by two less-than-reliable beacons: psychedelic drugs and the Eastern spiritual notion of the Third Eye.

The pineal is a tiny gland, the size of a grain of rice, located more or less in the dead centre of the brain. It was first described by the Greek anatomist Herophilus in around 300BC, after which its function was variously described in Galenic terms of humours and influences until, in the seventeenth century, it was elevated to the exalted state of the centre of consciousness by the philosopher René Descartes.

Descartes was particularly impressed by the fact that the pineal gland, unlike most brain organs, isn't one of a pair; this strongly suggested to him that it had to be the centre of something. He eventually conceived it as having two interlinking functions which, between them, spanned his dualistic divide of body and spirit. Its first role for him was as a filter or valve which controls the flow of thoughts into our consciousness — a theory very reminiscent of Huxley's classic account of psychedelic drug action in *Doors of Perception*. Its second role was "the seat of the soul" — or perhaps more graphically, the steering-wheel. His idea was that it's the instrument by which the invisible and material soul controls the brain, presenting the grey matter with thoughts which it's pre-selected from the realm of the spirit.

Clinical understanding of the pineal was initially pushed forward in modern times by the observation that certain lower vertebrates actually wear their pineal glands on the outside of their heads. The classic examples are the Western fence lizard, the Pacific tree-frog and the Pacific sea lamprey. In these creatures, the pineal gland is a literal third eye, positioned in the centre of the head and complete with cornea, rods and cones. It's not clear exactly what it sees — i.e. how the brain decodes its signal — but it suggested to scientists that the

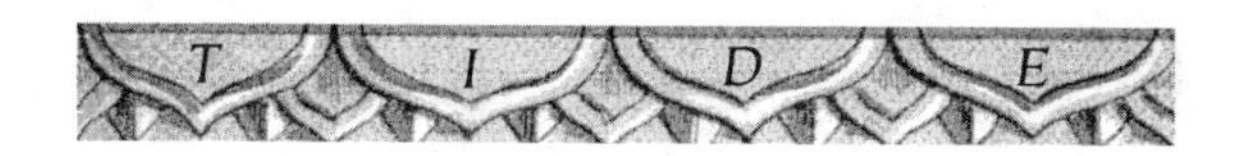

pineal glands of more developed animals may also be light-sensitive. This turned out to be the case with birds, whose pineals receive light and seem to be charged with setting their brains' diurnal and seasonal rhythms.

The revelation that the pineal is a form of eye drew obvious comparisons with the 'Third Eye,' the sixth chakra in the classical yoga system of Patanjali, which has been represented for many centuries as an eye in the centre of the forehead. This bolstered the claims of those who believed that yoga was an 'occult science' comparable to that of the West, though this was probably of more interest to Western converts than to Eastern practitioners, for whom the question of whether Western science agrees with them or not (it patently doesn't) was rather less pressing. Nevertheless, systems of correspondence began to emerge between the Eastern 'subtle body' and the Western model of brain and body interaction which is still being gradually assembled. The Third Eye and the pineal gland were usually pronounced to be one and the same, though some theorists, equating *prana* with the endocrine system, chose the pituitary gland instead.

Work on the pineal gland in mammals, meanwhile, showed that the more advanced they became, the more it receded into the brain, the less light it received and the less function it seemed to have. By the 1940s it had become virtually the appendix of the brain, a vestigial organ which had lost its usefulness during the course of our evolution. It was eventually rescued from atavistic obscurity, though, by the discovery of a substance which it alone produces: melatonin.

By the 1950s, studies on rodent reproductive cycles had demonstrated that melatonin is produced in the pineal gland at night and, for hibernating animals, controls the endocrine release which sets their body temperature and breeding seasons according to the amount of light in the day, thereby determining their deep, unconscious levels of body function. In humans, who don't hibernate, the levels being set by melatonin are more obscure. It's been associated with regulation of sleep, menstrual cycles and the onset of puberty.

But, beyond these, it seems also to control some deep levels of consciousness, in ways which are connected with the complex chemical cycle by which melatonin is produced. It's manufactured from serotonin, which is broken down into tryptamines and beta-carbolines — the endo-*ayahuasca* brew — before becoming melatonin. Various complexes of tryptamines and harmala alkaloids, as metabolites of this process, cycle round the pineal as levels of melatonin rise and fall.

The effects of these substances in the pineal is even less clear than those of melatonin. They seem to be implicated in the maintaining of REM sleep, and thus directly affect the dreaming process — perhaps accounting for the similarity between *harmal* visions and lucid dreams. They have the effect of inhibiting the breakdown of serotonin, and thus increase the amount of serotonin in the brain — the basic *modus operandi* of most psychedelic drugs. And, most tentatively, dramatically high levels of them seem to be pumped out during the classic 'near death experience' — which frequently involves hallucinations of a tunnel, a bridge, 'spirit guides' to the beyond, and the parade of shamanic imagery so specifically recounted in the *Arda Wiraz Namaq*. After death, the necrosis of the pineal gland produces a chemical breakdown far richer in psychedelic compounds that while the brain's alive.

Another response associated with the near-death experience is particularly interesting to me. The shifting neurotransmitter levels associated with this particular pineal action often cause what's known as a 'myotonic twitch,' a reflex action of the spine at the base of the skull. This is definitely the tugging sensation which I've now felt several times, and for which I've heard several explanations. Practitioners of astral projection are familiar with it, describing it as the sensation of the astral body tugging loose from the physical. The Bwiti people of West Africa, who use a plant root called ibogaine to make 'spirit journeys' in some ways similar to those accessible on harmaline, call this effect "the splitting of the skull"; for them it's the defining moment in the experience where the subject enters the realm of the ancestors. Its proximity to near-death responses also makes me wonder whether it's responsible for the presence of death often described in harmaline visions by Skip, Naranjo and others.

Beyond these suppositions, one of the clearest facts about the action of the pineal gland is that it's affected by psychedelic drugs — and, anecdotally, also by meditation and various yogi states, where melatonin increases are said to have been measured in appropriately-wired yogis who've subjected themselves to scientific testing. It's full of the specific receptors for tryptamines and beta-carbolines which both the classic pyschedelics and the harmala alkaloids slot into, and its action is significantly boosted by the introduction of these substances across the blood-brain barrier. Whatever it is that the pineal gland does, whatever deep conscious or unconscious states it generates, are pushed from the mind's shadows into the foreground by substances like harmaline and *ayahuasca*. Worlds of dreams or death, perhaps, where the part of the brain which is most alien to our normal consciousness takes the stage, and shows us in vivid detail things which are normally lost, far in the background noise of waking life.

Gordon Hillman, whose interest has been fired by the news of *harmal's* psychoactive properties, has been keeping an eye out for anyone else who may be working along similar lines. He passes on to me the email address of a botanist who's working in Israel named Aref Abu-Rabia. Aref is a Bedouin by birth who's been studying the use of plants by the nomadic Bedouin of the

Negev desert. He's sure that there was some mention of *harmal*.

The Negev Bedouin turn out to be another anomaly in the Arab world, a people who've retained their traditional nomadic lifestyle since time immemorial. They regard themselves as the first Arabs, the descendents of Ishmael, Abraham's son, who stayed wandering in the desert after his brother Isaac chose to settle as a farmer with his people, the Hebrews. Abraham, the father of both races, is famously claimed as the father of monotheism, a title he shares with the less famous Zoroaster; unlike Zoroaster, though, the Abraham of the Bible is a composite, mythic character who left no writings behind him. But the Bedouin have undoubtedly retained many elements of their culture from a similarly distant antiquity.

Aref replies to my message the next day, courteously addressing me as "Doctor." Yes, he's become particularly interested in the Negev Bedouin use of *harmal* and has followed it up on several research trips. No, he was unaware of its historical provenance, or the existence of a harmaline-containing plant in the New World.

There's a general conspiracy theory in the drug subculture that academics don't want to take drugs seriously, and suppress research relating to them. My experience up to this point has been entirely the opposite. All the ones I've approached have been helpful and open-minded beyond my wildest expectations. My feeling is that the opposite is true: far from suppressing drug research, they're unable to collate it all themselves. Drugs are such a multidisciplinary subject, and professional academics are so specialised, they're unable to put all the pieces together. Rather than hollering 'conspiracy,' the interested drug users of the world could perhaps more profitably be out there doing this job themselves, rather than waiting for the academics to do it for them.

Aref's story is fascinating. It started when he noticed that the Negev would occasionally throw a handful of *harmal* seeds in with their cattle-feed. When he asked them about this, they

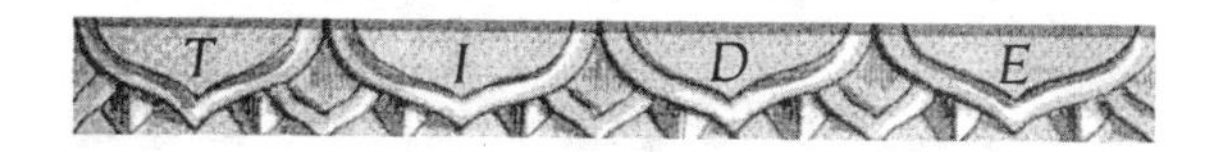

told him it was a fertility treatment, used when their cattle weren't calving enough.

It turned out that its use in fertility wasn't limited to cattle. *Harmal* is also mixed with olive oil and other substances, usually by healers and with techniques which are handed down from father to son. Men and women both use this potion in order to become pregnant. Fertility is another property which bonds *harmal* and *haoma*. The Zoroastrian *Yasna* hymns of worship tell that *"Haoma grants pregnant women kingly sons and righteous progeny,"* and there are many other similar refences. On a metaphorical level, this can be explained by the association of *haoma* with plant life, water, rain, the moon and generally the feminine aspects of creation. But *harmal's* continued reputation for fertility across the Arab world suggests that, as so often, the metaphorical and the literal may be inextricably interwoven.

It's also regarded as an aphrodisiac and, conversely, sometimes used as an abortifacient for unwanted pregnancy — after, as Aref puts it, *"boyfriend or romantic 'incident' in the desert."* I've come across this in other shreds of botanical literature, and found it confusing: how can *harmal* promote both fertility and miscarriage? Doesn't this just suggest that the plant is regarded in some fuzzy and entirely non-medical way as 'good for everything'?

In fact, I find an entirely satisfactory resolution to this apparent contradiction in the work of the eminent underground chemist Alexander Shulgin. He's recently experimented both with synthesized harmaline and with extractions from the seeds of *harmal*, and has analysed the *harmal* samples for traces of other active ingredients. Besides harmaline, harmine and the other beta-carbolines, he's noticed that *harmal* also contains small amounts of another entirely unrelated alkaloid called vasicine, which is indeed used as an abortifacient in animals. For what it's worth, the traditional Bedouin remedy passes the acid test of science.

But, as well as its medical uses, Aref notes that *harmal* is also used for its psychoactive effects. The Bedouin burn the seeds, like many Arab and Iranian people, but inhale the smoke after the manner of the ancient Scythians and, according to Aref's description, for similar reasons: *"to have illusions and to be in high spirits."*

I'm surprised that they manage to inhale an effective amount of the smoke, since my experiments suggested that this was more or less impossible. Aref explains that they inhale the smoke into their stomachs, and exhale it slowly through the nose. This presumably allows it to be absorbed through the stomach wall and various internal membranes; interestingly, this technique is also used in the Amazon for amplifying the psychotropic effects of tobacco. Smoke is swallowed into the stomach, allowed to circulate for several minutes and then impressively belched up some time later.

Among the Bedouin, though, *harmal's* psychoactive use is more than purely recreational. It's also used ritually in healing ceremonies which even Aref, though a Bedouin himself, isn't allowed to witness. Healers administer it, as far as he can gather, to people with what we would call various mental disorders — *"despair, depression, weakness, Alzheimer's disease."* This is a one-on-one healing ritual performed in seclusion, and presumably resembling in some respects Naranjo's harmaline psychotherapy.

A people with many traditions which have persisted unchanged from prehistory, the Negev Bedouin offer the first documented example I've come across of contemporary use of *harmal* as an intoxicant. I begin to wonder how much more of it there might be out there.

5

JUNGLE JUICE

By happy coincidence, a major conference on Zoroastrian literature is taking place in London. All the most eminent Zoroastrian scholars will be there, including Martin Schwartz, co-author of *Haoma and Harmaline,* and many others whose books I've been reading. This will be the perfect opportunity to try and find some kind of consensus on the identity of *haoma*.

The conference takes place in Zoroastrian House, a detatched Victorian building in a leafy North London street which I've walked past several times without being aware that it was a public building at all, let alone the British headquarters of the world's oldest synoptic religion. Inside, it feels like a parochial church hall, with wooden parquet floors, moulded ceilings, trestle tables of tea and biscuits.

The hundred or so people who are milling around divide conspicuously into two camps: Zoroastrians and Avestan scholars. The Zoroastrians are a mixture of Iranians, many of whom have been living in the West since the 1979 revolution, and Parsees from India, the Zoroastrians who were driven east after the Islamic conquest of Iran a thousand years ago and who have formed a tightly-knit, doctrinally traditionalist wing of the religion centred mostly in Bombay. Together, they form a loud, colourful and friendly crowd. The Avestan scholars, on the other hand, are predominantly elderly white male academics who seem to be only marginally interested in the Zoroastrianism of today. They represent a kind of apex of the Western academic specialisation which has grown out of the Sanskrit scholarship initiated by Sir William Jones two centuries ago, and which up until this century was the vanguard of academic philology and linguistic studies. But while the mainstream of linguistics since the war has shifted its focus to Piaget and Chomsky, neurolinguistics and cognitive psychology, these few have progressed from Sanskrit to Avestan throughout a lifetime of specialisation in a demanding but dwindling academic field.

As almost the only person here who conspicuously isn't either a Zoroastrian or an Avestan scholar, I'm an object of some curiosity. Flamboyant and gossipy women in sarees approach me, make me feel welcome, ask what my interest is, make sure I'm issued with meal tickets and programmes and point out the various luminaries to me.

As the lectures begin, the gulf between Zoroastrians and academics moves to centre stage. The Zoroastrians form the audience, listening patiently as a procession of elderly German, Italian and British men discuss text stemmas, codices and Sogdian dialects, and compare various translations of single lines of the *Gathas*.

Their patience, though, is sporadically well rewarded. Professor Kaikhosrov Irani from the City University in New York, a philosopher with a bow-tie, goatee beard and crowd-pleasing dry humour, offers us his "three stages of religion." First is shamanism — what he calls "ancient technology," the practise of elemental magic by individual ordeal. Second is priesthood — a formal and social arrangement between man and god, based on ritual sacrifice. Third is 'reflective' religion — supra-tribal, based on personal choice, consent and lifestyle: this last, 'modern' religion, is Zoroaster's gift to the world, his contribution to human history.

This type of schema has been formulated many times from the first sociologists of religion like Emile Durkheim onwards. Related systems also abound: for example, describing the changing relationships between magic, religion and science as societies develop. Most of them offer a trade-off between a broad, helpful framework and various fuzzy edges and facts that don't fit: both of these become apparent when I chat to Professor Irani afterwards about how *haoma* fits into his scheme. He acknowledges that it's a little problematic, for two reasons. First, in the time before Zoroaster, the *haoma* cult ('stage one') seems to have co-existed with the Magian priesthood ('stage two'). Second, although Zoroastrianism forms the most perfect illustration of the three stages, it did actually regress to 'stage two' after Zoroaster ushered in 'stage three'. In other words, after the elective, personal religious statement of the *Gathas,* a stage-two priesthood coalesced again around Zoroaster's teaching, re-instituting a watered-down form of the 'ancient technology' of the *haoma* cult ('stage one') with the psychedelic core, of course, omitted.

In a way, this is an explanation so confusing that we might feel that the story was clearer before the explanation; but it's an analysis which at least makes clear that the development of religions is often hard to reduce to linear form, and that most living religions are in fact many different stages of 'evolution' co-existing rather illogically side by side.

Stanley Insler, from Yale, also has some interesting insights into Zoroaster's contribution to human history. The effect of his 'abstraction' of the Magian symbols and rituals was, he suggests, to allow people to think for themselves. Fire isn't just fire but is also truth; cattle are cattle but also 'good thought': all this shows that man and god, sacred and profane, are really two aspects of

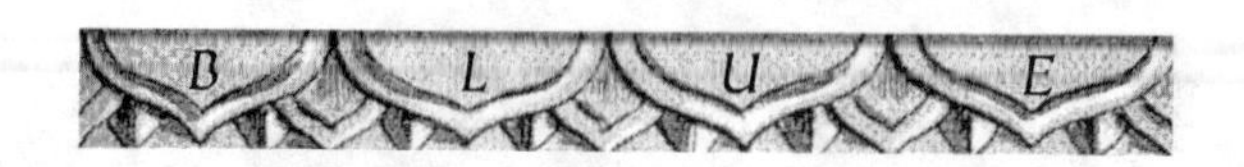

the same thing. This means that man's communion with god no longer has to take the form of prescribed and ordained sacrifice, but can take place in the heart of any man simply by 'good thought, good words, good deeds'.

This is where Zoroaster stands in such strong contrast to the parallel and contemporary Vedic tradition. The same process took place later in India: the sacred ground of a sacrifice eventually came to be seen as a representation of the universe in microcosm, but only after several more centuries of sterile, rule-bound sacrificial rites. Zoroaster's contribution jumped the gun by hundreds of years, ushering in something modern while the human race was still at the dawn of history. This is why the religion regressed to a priesthood again after his death, and this is also the reason why Zoroaster's contribution is so hard to focus on down the long corridor of antiquity.

Stanley Insler and I work our way through a pack of cigarettes on the steps outside. He's wry, witty and utterly charming. He talks about how much we can tell of Zoroaster's character from the *Gathas* — his love of horses, for example. I ask him about *haoma,* and what he thinks its botanical identity was.

"It's got to be ephedra. Obviously. Syrian Rue? How can you have a religious ritual on a psychedelic? You wouldn't remember anything. Anyway, we know all about ephedra. *Hom. The Hom Yasht*. I mean, what's to look for? They still use it today."

I wander in for lunch, and find myself sitting next to Martin Schwartz. I tell him I've been following up on *Haoma and Harmaline*. He asks if I'm convinced by his thesis. I tell him, I think it's certainly the most interesting. I ask him if he still stands by it.

"Oh, it has to be Syrian Rue. Obviously. The linguistic argument is so compelling. It's still the same word, for Chrissakes."

Browsing at the makeshift bookstall, I bump into Dr. Ali Jafarey, the head of the Zoroastrian Religious Assembly in San Diego. Dr. Jafarey, a convert to Zoroastrianism, pushes a

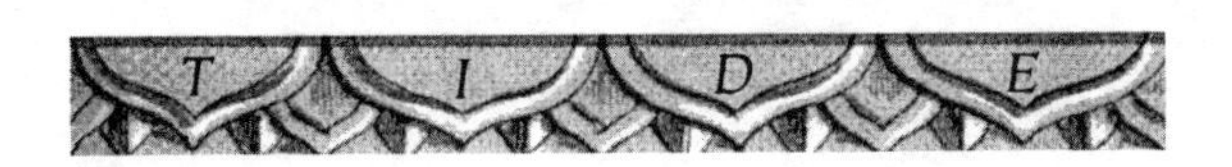

modern, ecumenical line. He regards Zoroaster's *Gathas* as the unmediated word of the Prophet, passed down to us across the centuries, and has translated them into fluent modern English. He views the later Zoroastrian sacred texts, the *Avestas,* the *Vendidad* and so on, simply as priestly rule-books, extraneous to the divine message. This sets him at loggerheads with the more traditionally-minded Bombay Parsees. I've tuned into some of these heated exchanges on the net, and he remembers my questions about *haoma*. I ask him his view.

"It's obviously cannabis. Hemp. I mean, I've been to India, seen them making *bhang* exactly as described, sieved through the cloth, mixed with milk. It's no mystery. The tradition is unchanged. There's nothing even to look for."

Across the room, I spot the eminence grise of Avestan scholarship, the incredibly distinguished Dr.Ilya Gershevitch, who founded the department of Iranian Studies at Cambridge in 1948 and, now in his eighties, is still incumbent at Jesus College. I'm aware that he's written a paper on *soma/haoma*, but have never been able to track it down. I approach him tentatively with my request, and he tells me he'll send a copy. I give him my address.

I await it with interest, dying to see if there's even the slightest hint of consensus among these brilliantly able men who've spent most of their lives trying to unravel these mysteries. I briefly entertain the fantasy of getting them all together for a week and insisting that they all try all of the drugs in question. I wonder if it would change their minds.

☆ ☆

Dr. Gershevitch's paper arrives the next week with a charming cover-note. Like his lecture, it's a magnificent piece of micro-scholarship, arguments and textual passages dissected as if with a diamond scalpel in a kid-gloved hand. It takes me about half an hour before I can follow his argument closely enough to see what plant he's suggesting. In fact, he follows Wasson's line, suggesting fly agaric. The lack of consensus is total.

But his paper does turn up something crucial, something which I'd suspected but never seen proved before. In some of the inscriptions of Darius and Xerxes, a nomadic people living on the northern borders of the Iranian world, around Tashkent, are described as the "*haoma*-drinkers." These are likely to have been the Tura people of higher antiquity, people who stemmed from the same Indo-Iranian roots of Indra-worship but who remained nomadic after the 'Avestan' people settled. But the Avestan Iranians themselves were *haoma*-drinkers, albeit of the substitute *haoma* which was probably *hom* — ephedra. So to refer to another tribe as *haoma*-drinkers suggests that *haoma,* at least at certain times, referred to more than one plant.

This is proof positive of a hypothesis which has come to seem more and more likely to me: that *soma*, and *haoma,* could have referred to different plants, or plant-combinations, at different times and in different places. This is clearly true of the bewildering complex of *soma*- and *haoma*-substitutes which seem to have come into use in both Vedic and Iranian traditions both before and after the original psychedelic was 'lost,' 'banned' or otherwise fell into disuse — and various of which are still in use today. But is it possible also that the original *soma* and *haoma* were not so much a single plant as a complex of various sacred intoxicants? Or, perhaps, that the mixture drunk by the priests differed from that offered to the worshippers? Or, perhaps, that *soma* and *haoma* represented different admixtures of the same family of ingredients?

☆ ☆

I ponder Stanley Insler's objection that it's not possible to have a religious ritual on a psychedelic. I'm inclined to agree with him as far as most classic major psychedelics go, providing that we distinguish between shamanic trance or possession — where major psychedelics are commonly used — and a priestly group ritual. But, even in this second category, I'm inclined to think that *harmal* is a plausible sacrament. First, because the specificity of its visions makes it uniquely possible to share a group experience. Second, because its peculiar qualities of stimulating imagery without loss of control would allow its subjects to take part in a reasonably complex and formal religious ceremony without becoming confused and incapacitated.

More broadly, I find myself considering the relationship between drug use and organised religion. *Soma*, after all, is a prime example of the fact that plant drug 'sacraments' lie at the ultimate roots of most of the great world religions. But, today, drugs and religion sit uncomfortably together. Religion and drug use both typically demonise the other, but it seems to me that they're not opposed to each other in spiritual intent; on the contrary, it's more as if they're too close to one another, somehow fighting over the same patch. Both offer the possibility of connecting us in some way with the eternal and divine; but do they in fact take us to the same place?

Most religions insist, one way or another, that they don't. Zoroaster's injunction to end the *"filthy intoxication"* of *haoma* seems to have trickled, along with Good and Evil, Heaven and Hell, down into the roots of Judaism, Christianity and Islam. All have more or less institutionalised prohibitions against drug use, despite any overt references to it in their sacred texts.

In Christianity, its basis is in passages like the drunkenness of Noah, even though Christianity, developing in an alcohol-fuelled culture and traditionally revolving around an alcohol-based sacrament, has tended to relegate alcoholic abstinence to its more ascetic margins. In Islam, alcohol is of course forbidden, but there's no reference to hashish or opium intoxication in the Koran. The widespread disapproval of drugs in the Arab world is explained in terms of reason, which is the greatest gift of God to man: it's reason which separates man from the animals, and so to cast it aside voluntarily amounts to blasphemy. Nevertheless, the use of hashish and opium (and *harmal?*) as routes to divine ecstasy have been practised for centuries in various heretical sufi traditions. The *hadith,* or sayings of the Prophet, do include a specific injunction not to pray while intoxicated: the heterodox sufi interpretation of this is that to reach a state of divine intoxication is itself equal to prayer, and that the true meaning of the *hadith* is that those who are truly intoxicated don't need to pray. And despite the prolific use of *bhang* and ganja by Indian saddhus, most organised Eastern religions proclaim that they're offering all that's needed to attain enlightenment, and the use of drugs is misguided and unnecessary.

By and large, though, drugs and religion remain in almost polar opposition in the modern world, proponents of each viewing them as alternatives to the other. Drug addicts are 'saved' by Jesus and born again as Christians; less frequently, perhaps, trainee priests try LSD and leave their seminaries, wondering why they wasted all that time. Specifically, religious groups have been in the militant forefront of this century's prohibition of drugs. It was under pressure from Catholic missionaries that Governor Taft of the Philippines, the United States' only colony, brought in the first ever national prohibition of opium in 1900 — the same year, ironically, that Bayer Pharmaceuticals launched heroin as an over-the-counter medicine.

It's easier to attest the presence of this recurring pattern than it is to account for it. The 'first stage' of religion is characterised by many elements — tribal unity, cultic ritual and, in almost every case, the use of plant drugs. Psychoactive plants are present in the indigenous cultures of every continent of the world. Seeds — *harmal,* datura, morning glory — are smoked and swallowed. Roots — *kava* in Polynesia, *iboga* in West Africa — are mashed, brewed and drunk. Cacti are skinned, vines are peeled, mushroom buttons are dried, smoked and chewed. In every case the consumption of these plants is inextricably connected with the most sacred religious practices. The 'power plants' are revered as the kings and queens of nature, where the quintessence of the Other World has been concentrated and made available to man as the ultimate bounty of the gods.

By contrast, our notional 'second stage' of religion — an evolved and hierarchical priesthood which is also a complex administrative power-base — is characterised by the almost compete absence of these plants of power. In Zoroastrianism, Judaism, Christianity, Islam — the Religions of the Book — their use is either specifically outlawed (usually by later, specific interpretations of earlier, vaguer texts) or culturally ostracised. In the Hindu, Buddhist, Sikh, Jain and other related traditions their use is sporadically and locally tolerated but never officially sanctioned. The religious propaganda which has led the War on Drugs this century has constructed a monolithic exclusion of drug use at the most fundamental level, painting it as delusional, hedonistic, diseased, a hubristic attempt to storm heaven with chemical weapons which can only ever be rewarded with the nemesis of physical, moral and spiritual ruin.

To the drug counterculture which has emerged in the modern West, this dramatic contrast has increasingly come to be explained by an alternative history which, like most alternative histories, derives its force from the postulation of a hidden conspiracy. Drugs, so the argument goes, offer the most direct and personal route to the divine realm. As such they limit the authority of the priestcraft to mediate and control the religious experience of their people effectively: the priests can only establish a monopoly over the drug, and not over the world to which the drug takes the worshipper. Once drugs have been (by hook or by crook) got rid of, then the priests find themselves presiding over a flock with no rival path to heaven.

This leaves them free to devise a monopoly of their own choosing and design it to serve their own best interests.

This may well represent a dynamic, conscious or unconscious, in the process, but it's unconvincing as its sole *raison d'être*. First, like most conspiracy theories, it requires us to believe in an elite motivated solely by evil intent. Second, it requires that everyone else has acquiesced like sheep in this new arrangement. It's hard to imagine that the early Hindus would have submitted to the dictates of Brahmins demanding that they jump through authoritarian hoops in order to drink something that wasn't even *soma*, unless the true *soma* genuinely had been in some way 'lost,' in the sense that the original experience was no longer available to them.

The alternative history explains this loss in terms of, effectively, a dualistic struggle between good and evil. Primitive humans, according to various recent theories, divided into two types: the peaceful, wise, goddess-worshipping drug-takers and the macho, conflict-obsessed, alcohol-drinking warriors. It was these latter who came to prevail as we emerged into history, particularly in the West through the agency of the Roman Empire and Christianity.

The problem with this interpretation is well-illustrated by the Vedic *soma*-drinkers, probably the classic example of Golden Age drug cultists but also a culture of aggressive, illiterate, barbarian robber-barons who sustained a proto-feudal system by pitiless force which involved, among other things, the suppression and effective destruction of the more civilised, literate Dravidian agriculturalists who had the misfortune to be in their way. More generally, very few ancient societies seem to correspond with any accuracy to either stereotype. The feminised drug-takers and the alcoholic warriors, if they're anything, are modes which all cultures display on different levels. More than anything, though, this division seems to represent the current social disjunction between 'hippies' and 'straights' projected backwards onto prehistory.

But perhaps we can construct a broader, more complex story where the 'loss' of the divine plants came about as an effect of something else, rather than being the both the cause and effect of priestly repression. For this, Zoroaster serves as our paradigmatic example: his new dispensation may not have been designed specifically to destroy the *haoma* cult but, fixed as it was on a dazzling new vision of the future, it would naturally tend to marginalise those parts of his tradition which were the bastions of ancestral worship and the mythical Golden Age which he was trying to replace with an apocalyptic teleology.

But there are other reasons why the power of plant drugs might tend to wane, with or without these elite priestly manoeuvres. As Manuel Cordoba de Rios' experiences with *ayahuasca* in the Amazon demonstrate, the power of a drug like *ayahuasca* in a shamanic society resides largely in its extraordinary ability to feed off a 'group mind' which allows all the drug's subjects to be transported into a shared Other World so highly consensual that it verges, by our definition, into telepathy. If an increasingly structured priesthood was developed by the extension of a culture out from its original tribal base into a broader collective of peoples, then it's unlikely that this shared world of drug experience would sustain its potency in quite the same way as before. With a fractured collective consciousness, a canonical standard of priestly wisdom might naturally become a more reliable form of transmission than the drug-based rituals from which it sprung. 'The book' would reach parts that 'the drug' no longer could.

So, as religions grew, the drug might indeed become 'lost' — not in the sense of the plant becoming extinct, but simply because the drug, as a key to the divine, simply no longer worked in the way in which it had originally done in the time of the ancestors. We can imagine this process taking place as Zoroaster's reforms took hold — reforms which were specifically focused on drawing out the abstract and universal qualities of what had previously been a tribal, cultic complex of beliefs.

There are a handful of exceptions to this disjunction between drugs and religion but, in one way or another, most of them are exceptions which on closer inspection confirm the rule. The most obvious one which occurs to me is the use of ganja as a sacrament in the Rastafarian Church: only when I look into it do I discover that it's not a sacrament at all. The canonical Ethiopian Orthodox church don't use ganja at all, and the origins of its use (as the name ganja suggests) are among the Hindu community who emigrated to Jamaica after the abolition of slavery. The ganja-smoking Rastafari adopted many habits of Indian saddhus: the ascetic life, wandering in the hills or living in informal camps, and smoking ganja in the chillum-style pipe originally consecrated to Shiva. As a result, the mainstream Rastafarian churches tolerate the use of ganja among holy men without sanctioning it; it's informally associated with the "green herb" of the King James bible, and qualified as an "incense pleasing to the Lord."

This broad mainstream tolerance did, however, provide the springboard for a splinter church to try to institutionalise ganja as a central sacrament. The Zion Coptic Church, a Garveyite orthodox denomination with Gnostic leanings, had a small membership which was declining until the mid-sixties, when it was revitalised by white Rasta converts and institutionalised the ritual consumption of ganja with a bizarre, lengthy and fascinating document of real and imagined Biblical references to drug-taking. This provoked a landmark church-state case which landed several of the Coptics' leader in prison, a pattern which was to recur sporadically with other drug-based new religious movements.

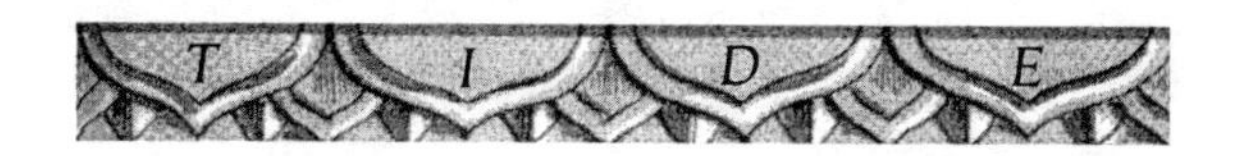

The most conspicuous and successful combination of drug use and religion this century is probably the Native American Church, the Christian pan-tribal organisation which uses peyote cactus as its central sacrament with — after several decades of bitter struggle — little current interference from US federal or state law. This, too, is an exception which confirms the rule, but in a different way.

The origin of the Native American Church can be largely traced to the short-lived Ghost Dance religion, a millenarian movement which spread rapidly across many North American tribes, including the Sioux, Wichita, Apache and Arapaho, in the 1890s, after the massacre at Wounded Knee. It combined both traditional Paiute beliefs in the periodic renewal of the world and missionary teachings of the Second Coming of Jesus into a belief that the remaking of the world was at hand, and the new century would see the European invaders quietly removed and the Native Americans once more restored to their former state.

The main focus of this religion was a dance which was continued for five nights in succession, during which many people fell into trances, had communion with their dead relatives and received channelled information about the coming End Times. Most tribes believed that the transition would be non-violent, and were unnervingly restrained towards the whites, teaching that the tribes should treat the white man with discretion and politeness since he was about to be destroyed in the floods and fires of the imminent apocalypse.

As it ebbed, it left a significantly altered state of things in its wake. First, inter-tribal communications and networks had been much strengthened, allowing them to come together to develop pan-Indian ideas more freely. Second, they had united behind a syncretic mixture of traditional Native and new Christian beliefs. Third, the trade and exchange routes which had been developed came to be trodden by wandering medicine men, many of them bringing the peyote cactus and its attendant rituals from Mexico to the Northern States for the first time.

In the years that followed, the traditional peyote ritual, in its variant forms of the 'half-moon' and 'full-moon' ceremonies, spread across the United States in tandem with an adopted form of Christianity which associated the Indian view of the cactus as "God's flesh" with the transubstantiation of Christ's body in the communion and the doctrine of the Holy Spirit. Early peyote-men like the splendidly-named John Rave baptised new members in the name of the Father, the Son and the Holy Ghost while making a cross on the convert's head with peyote-juice. This development aroused the horror of many Christian missionaries, and state laws against the trafficking in peyote buttons were sporadically passed and enforced. Efforts to pass a federal law against peyote use began as early as 1912, and the tribes were forced to make a co-ordinated attempt to resist it. In 1918 they formed the Native American Church, with official articles which both enshrined the peyote rite as its central sacrament and offered it protection under the constitutional right of freedom to worship. Efforts to prohibit the Church's use of peyote continued through to the 1980s, by which time enough precedents had been set for their rights to be more or less secured.

The Native American Church is a bona-fide example of an organised religion centred around the use of a psychedelic plant, but one in which the opposing poles of drug use and religious organisation are clearly in conflict: its incorporation as an organised religion can be seen as a defence mechanism against organised state religion itself. It's a story of bitter conflict and harrassment, but ultimately one of success — a success which many have attempted to emulate, but which no other group has attained. Particularly after the psychedelic evangelising of Timothy Leary in the 1960s and 1970s, several groups of spiritually-orientated drug users — the Neo-American

Church, the True Temple of Inner Light and others — have attempted to enshrine their practices in a religious structure, but most, like the Zion Coptics, have ended up on the losing side in court. The gist of most of the judgements is that they actually constitute a group of like-minded individuals indulging in drug use, rather than a religion.

I'm glad someone can tell the difference.

☆ ☆

While I'm following this line of research, I come across a drug-based religion which not only seems to break all the rules: it also does so with harmaline.

I discover on the internet the existence of a Christian Church in Brazil which uses *ayahuasca* as a sacrament: the Church of Santo Daime. The Church of Santo Daime's own literature is highly Christian in tone, with an almost Pentecostal fervour. It makes no reference to the use of drugs — only to the 'Daime,' its unspecified sacrament. Gathering a little more context, I discover that the Church has been growing rapidly in Brazil, especially over the last twenty years, and is beginning to extend worldwide. It's most popular in the large urban areas, and among first- or second-generation displaced people from the jungles and villages, for whom it functions as a community with strong links to Brazil's Indian roots. Its sacrament, the 'Daime,' is an *ayahuasca* brew, made in the traditional Indian manner with varying proportions of harmaline-containing *yage* vine and DMT sources such as the leaves of the fast-growing jungle shrub *psychotria viridis.*

The ceremonies are by all accounts fairly intense and powerful affairs, but probably less conspicuously so in a country like Brazil where various forms of syncretic and shamanic trance and spirit possession — umbanda, kandombleh and so on — are, along with ecstatic music and pervasive Catholic and pagan rituals, part of daily life. The services, weekly or fortnightly, tend to start at sunset and often go on all night.

Several ethnologists, psychologists and drug researchers have attended Santo Daime ceremonies, and a few of them have written reports on their experiences. Following these up, I discover that the Church has recently expanded beyond Brazil. Several *padrinhos,* as the church leaders are called, have visited Europe, initially Spain and Portugal, but subsequently various Mediterranean spots such as Ibiza. Now there's even an active church in Amsterdam.

This strikes me as a wildly unexpected chance to answer many of my questions. How are the visions of *ayahuasca* channelled among a group of worshippers? How does the *ayahuasca* ritual work when transplanted into a Christian ceremony? How is the solitary, withdrawn nature of the experience squared with the group dynamics of a shared religious experience?

I track down one of the participants on the net, who offers to forward a letter from me to the Church. I tell them briefly that I've been working with *harmal,* that I'm very interested in learning from them, that I'm prepared to travel to Amsterdam or somewhere in Europe if necessary.

A couple of days later, I get a call from a lady called Iko, who runs the local Santo Daime Church. There's a branch in North London.

Harmal, Zoroastrians, now the Church of Santo Daime: they all seem to be appearing on my doorstep.

☆ ☆

I'm invited to turn up for an 'orientation' into the Church a few days in advance of the 'work,' which is taking place on Sunday night, at the full moon. Generally, the ceremonies seem to run fortnightly, along the old and new moons.

The Church is an end-of-terrace house where Iko lives with Jimmy, her partner, and their young kid. We leave our shoes at the door and are shown into an upstairs front room, decorated with framed photos of long-bearded Brazilian *padrinhos*, Christian iconography and some instantly recognisable symbolist images — stars, moons and night panoramas — drawn from the Daime visions.

I learn that the Church was founded in the 1930s by a seven-foot-tall black Brazilian rubber-tapper named Raimundo Irineu Serra, known to the Church as Master Irineu. He encountered a tribe of *ayahuasca*-drinkers while working in the Amazon, and decided to fast for eleven days on manioc and then take it alone in the jungle. When he did so, he met the Queen of the Forest, who became the central icon of the Church; in true syncretic Brazilian fashion, she's also the Virgin Mary and, in an echo of the original *Soma*, lives on the moon. In the course of his 'work' with *ayahuasca*, Master Irineu chanelled 128 hymns, music and lyrics together, which form the core spiritual texts of the Church. He also renamed the *ayahuasca* brew the Daime, from the Portugese for "give me": many of the hymns ask for God to "give me" Love, Light and Strength.

The religion has grown by personal transmission, Master Irineu introducing other worshippers who in turn become *padrinhos*, channelling their own hymns. The number of hymns is constantly growing, passing round the world in photocopied and cone-bound samizdat volumes. Iko shows us some of these: every Church has a library of them. They're illustrated with some very distinctive *harmal* visions: woodcuts of cities on mountains, under night skies of big moons and stars.

Iko was involved in Buddhism and then with Native American sweat lodge work before she came to Santo Daime. If you join the Church, you get a 'star,' wear ceremonial costumes and are brought into the network of channelled hymns and travelling *padrinhos*. The main symbols of the Church are a quarter moon, a star and an eagle. She's been

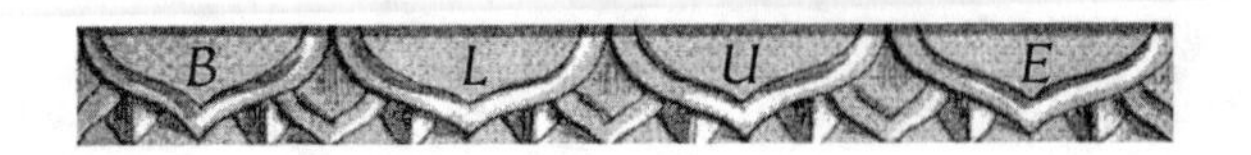

charged with setting up this new London group. There are already churches in Holland, Germany, Switzerland, France and Spain — they always thought that Britain would be the last to catch on. Apart from America, of course: there have been groups in California and Washington State, but they've run into legal difficulties. The States is the only nation which prohibits religious ayahuacsa use.

She explains the cosmology of the Church as a mixture of Christian and 'elemental'. Christianity is represented by a cross on the centre of the altar, the saying of Our Fathers and Hail Marys, and the insistence that participants cross themselves before taking the Daime. A glance at the photocopied literature shows more traces of insidious Christianisation: we're told that the traditional Indian name for the brew is "the wine of the soul," with its echoes of Holy Communion, rather than "the vine of the soul," which is how *'ayahuasca'* actually translates. The 'elemental' entities include the Brazilian ocean-goddess Yemanja, the Queen of the Forest and many other animist deities. A Portugese girl asks if she'll see angels. The answer to that is yes, too.

Iko's description of the experience we can expect is fascinating. There's no reference to the Daime as a 'drug,' no use of the ubiquitous drug-culture term 'trip'. The whole experience is described in terms which are far more specific, and coined from a viewpoint which lacks all traces of mind-body dualism or scientific views of chemical action. The Daime itself is called the 'tea,' or just the Daime. It's prepared by the *padrinhos,* but they merely assist in the process: "the Daime makes the Daime." The tea combines the principles of Strength and Light, the harmaline in the *yage* vine representing the Strength, and the DMT-containing leaf the Light. Women sometimes sort the leaves, but the brew is always made by men. Iko apologises for the fact that, these days, it's brewed up in aluminium pots, rather than the traditional clay of the Indian shamans.

The ceremony itself is called the 'work' ("We're going to do a healing work..."). The effect of the drug is called the 'Current' ("We start to feel the current...," "while the current is strong..."). And the individual experience is called the 'pasasge' ("some of you may have a very strong passage..."). All these are, in fact, different senses of the generic word 'trip' which I'd never unpacked in this way before.

During the work, we'll come into contact with the spirits — some Christian, some elemental, some good, some bad. Celestial spirits, dangerous spirits, trickster spirits: this is the reason for the shared ritual, so that we can all help each other by focusing on the 'light,' and bringing down the positive spirits of Love, Light and Strength. Everyone must focus on the light, rising up to it, dealing with anything which tries to get in the way. Although the 'work' is shared, participants are encouraged to follow their own 'passages' and effectively ignore everyone else; despite this, the same spirits often appear to everyone — Iko recalls a work where everyone smelt the scent of geraniums which weren't there.

The subject of nausea and vomiting is also raised. Buckets are provided in case anybody feels the need to vomit: the explanation given is that strong physical responses are often part of the 'work,' the spirits telling you that you need to unblock your channels to make room for the teaching which they're bringing through. Although this is framed positively, it still makes me slightly uncomfortable, reminding me of Claudio Naranjo's view that, to put it crudely, the reason people throw up is because they aren't good Jungians. The physical cause of nausea and vomiting is that both the harmaline and the plant material in which it's suspended are toxic and emetic; while this isn't necessarily the whole truth, not telling it to people makes them feel, perhaps unfairly, that the nausea is somehow their fault. But within the spiritist view of what's going on, mentioning the toxicity of the Daime would clearly plant an unacceptably negative association in the minds of the participants.

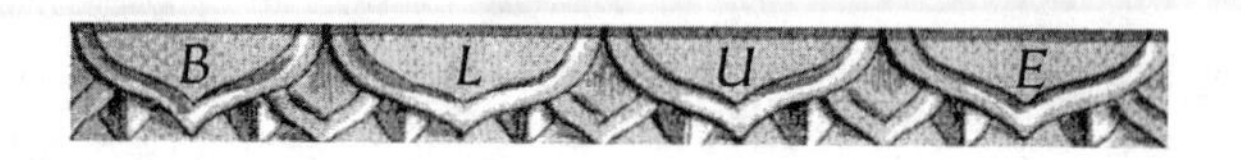

The Church asks for certain rules to be observed before, during and after the 'work'. Before and after the work, participants should abstain from alcohol and sex for about three days: the 'work' is about you and your personal energies, and they need to be fully charged and separated from your partner's. During the work, men and women are segregated. Participants should wear white or, failing that, any light colour. Red and black are to be avoided, having particularly negative energy. Of course, I'm wearing red and black. I mentally scour my wardrobe trying to remember if I own anything that isn't red or black.

Finally, they ask for a contribution of £30 for the costs of bringing the brew in. Considering they're offering a rare chance to experience one of life's most awesome possibilities on an extremely intimate basis to a group of virtual strangers, this seems more than reasonable.

☆ ☆

Sunday. I show up in the closest to white I can manage, after a couple of days of live yoghurt diet. We use the same room as before, but it's been rearranged with a table serving as an altar in the centre, and chairs around all four sides of it. There are about a dozen of us, probably two thirds male, mostly black or Portugese. We're seated carefully by Iko and Jimmy who are in their Santo Daime uniforms, white shirts, black bow ties and star badges, looking like the semi-divine cabin crew on a passenger flight to the beyond.

The ceremony begins with prayers and chanting. We stand up, sit down, stand up. After twenty minutes or so of blessings have been performed, Jimmy produces the Daime.

It's in a sealed glass bottle, brown, thick and opaque. Small tumblers are brought, and the brew is offered to each of us in turn. We cross ourselves before drinking it.

It's not as bitter as the *harmal* brew, though the underlying bitterness of harmaline is in there. But it's sour, like chyme, slightly fermented, with an overtone of rotting leaves. After all the *harmal,* the very fact that it's different is a relief, but it would be pretty hard on a delicate stomach. I focus on the taste as I swallow, imagining the process which is beginning inside me.

We sit down again, and the prayers continue. Iko produces some tapes of Brazilian Daime works, and sings along in a clear, powerful Portugese voice. I begin to feel the first responses, crawling skin, flashes at the edge of vision. Jimmy offers a second cup of the Daime. We all accept.

As soon as I drink the second cup, the first one starts to kick in. My stomach and spine tighten and loosen. An effervescence rises from my stomach into my head, my thoughts racing, as if I'm being dragged along by something fast and powerful.

Boy is there a lot of DMT in this brew. I realise that I've been expecting the wrong thing, imagining something meditative like the *harmal,* or the *ayahuasca* I had in Wales. This is going to be much more of a white-knuckle ride. I recognise the state of consciousness which is hurtling to meet me. It's probably analogous to a couple of hundred microgrammes of LSD, or a hundred psilocybin mushrooms. It's a state I enjoy enormously on an occasional basis, but one for which I'm in the habit of choosing my own setting very carefully. Usually somewhere remote, surrounded by beautiful and benevolent nature. Not in someone else's front room, shoulder to shoulder with a bunch of strangers.

I have a brief flash of paranoia. I've been drugged! I'm at their mercy. What if they're about to run some Christian brainwashing control programme on me? What could I do?

I close my eyes, breathe deeply, listening to the music, concentrating on the effects of the brew. It's sublimely beautiful. The shuffling Latin beat behind the hymns oozes with the sensual effects of the intoxication. I find myself swaying, my spine like a vertical column of rippling light and

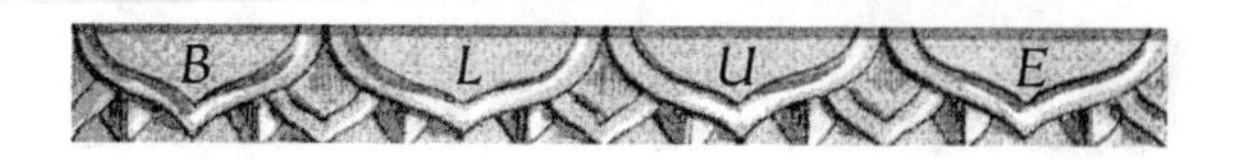

energy. I remember my earlier instructions and channel this energy out towards the altar. I feel as if I'm blasting it with waves of radiance, my muscles rippling out slowly and powerfully like a snake's.

The visions are beginning, and I recognise the moonlit blue sparks of the harmaline. But they're swamped by the full spectrum brilliance of the DMT, which is surging through me in intense rushes and leaving vivid tracers on my closed eyes. The harmonics of the music ripple out in vivid gossamer webs, like the scales of reptiles or fish, or bright sunlight reflected in oily water. It's like scuba-diving in a tropical reef made of pure light, with darting patterns of sentient life all around me.

I don't experience this in terms of spirits, entities or personalities. It feels more like an encounter with pure, protean energy, as if my life force has suddenly been cranked up to an area of the dial which most people don't know exists. I lose my residual discomfort with the Christian framework, which really boils down to Iko and Jimmy's belief that this energy is being visited on us from outside, whereas my firm belief — and unambiguous perception — is that it's coming from inside me. But who cares where it's coming from? This is *soma*, at least the metaphorical *soma*: the raw, unfiltered sensation of being alive, the dissolution of ego, the unmediated experience of what consciousness is and can be, the 'now' in all its polymorphous glory.

I open my eyes briefly, to see if everyone else is having the same experience. In my hypersensitised state, the sight is very freaky. Streamers of colour swirl across my vision, revealing a gallery of ruddy waxworks. Is this what humans really look like? Jimmy's eyes are closed, his chocolate skin smooth and suffused with ecstasy. He's absolutely solid gone, definitely in the place from which I've just surfaced. I feel the depth of his experience with this brew, his waves of unconditional love — of the Light, of Jesus, of all of us, of everything. His right to be the priest of

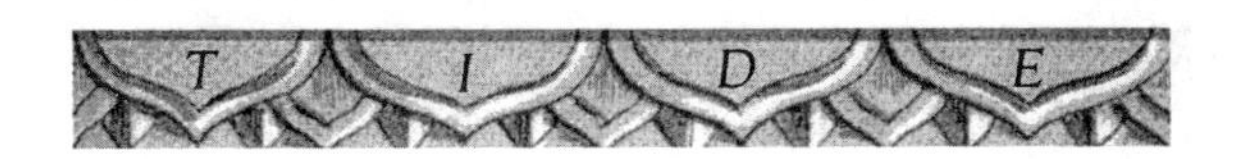

this ceremony is palpable, a right earned by ordeal: we're going to a place where he's been many times before, and we couldn't be in better hands.

But some of the rest of his congregation seem to be somewhere else altogether. The Portugese girl is sobbing, obviously caught up in something very personal and nightmarishly unresolvable. The man to the right of me is heaving up into his bucket; at the slightest effort, I can feel his stomach in peristalsis, his guts roiling. Mine start to do the same. I remember the instructions and tune out of his experience, closing my eyes again.

I'm aware of a great deal going on in the room. Everyone is, one way or another, in the grip of a very powerful experience. Various states of trance and possession: a couple of people are looking blissfully, angelically silent, hands clasped in prayer; others are huffing and swaying in some dark internal dialogue. I frequently have the very clear sensation that someone's leaving the room, brushing past the back of my chair as they go, but each time I open my eyes everyone's in their place.

As the initial surge of the Daime peaks and plateaus, I become more able to assemble my thoughts. The abstract realm of energy is still available, but now the workings of the mind are too. I descend from the apex of the primordial experience (the core of Professor Irani's 'stage one,' I recall incongruously), and engage in some reflection. Trains of thought surge through my mind, frequently contradictory, but in a way that seems irrelevant: opposites coexist without any lessening of their truth.

Basically, I think, what's going on here is just the action of the most sublime plant psychedelic. The Church is only framing the experience because it has a monopoly on the supply. If it was freely available, would I be sitting and doing this here? It's the old story: the priests are mediating an experience of the divine which at its root has nothing to do with them.

Then I think: these guys are simply going to clean up. They guarantee the most intense spiritual charge imaginable, something which all religions claim to offer but which none of the others can deliver with this overwhelming reliability. This is the only religious ceremony I've ever been to which actually takes you to the realm of the gods. I begin to consider the endless possibilities: different belief systems, different designer drugs perfectly tailored to the experience required, an alchemical marriage of chemistry and religion, a new age of scientific magic.

Then I think again: everything that's cosmically true and genuinely enlightening about this experience is coming from the Daime. The more I ignore the religious context, the more rewarding it is. But I'm sitting opposite Jimmy, whose serenity and focus are helping me so much to orientate my thoughts, to perceive it in the right way. Without Iko and Jimmy's guidance, and the imposition of the ritual, the rest of us would be doing...what exactly?

Then it occurs to me how much secular ritual we have in our lives, and how from this perspective the Daime ritual is just a heightened ceremonial version of the unconscious textures which run through much of normal life. The pervasive memes of drug culture are a good example of this. People often take psychedelics at sunset and piece together the events of the night at dawn, exactly the same pattern as the Santo Daime ceremonies. From rolling joints to injecting heroin, drug-taking is shot through with levels of ritual which are rarely this strictly formulated but are just as religiously adhered to.

The Daime rush falls off fast. It's probably been going on for about three hours. I've been sitting in a straight-backed wooden chair for about four hours, not crossing my arms or legs ("keep all your energy focused outwards towards the altar, don't withdraw from the group"), and I feel physically great: relaxed, enervated, as if I've been bathing in a hot spring. Jimmy checks that the 'current' is passing for everyone, and we stand up and kick the chairs back. Iko leads us in a dance to the music she's playing: an Indian three-step shuffle, very simple steps which I still find quite tricky in this state. The formation dancing makes us all connect for the first time, the basic coordination forging a group out of a bunch of very weirded-out individuals. Finally the ceremony is broken up, retracing our opening steps through the prayers and blessings.

Everyone — almost everyone — beams and smiles. We've been through a major ordeal together, and greet each other with a warmth which surprises us all. Iko and Jimmy make tea, and everyone hugs. A couple of the participants are still a little shaky, wanting time on their own. The Portugese girl abandoned her chair some way into the ceremony and is still lying in a corner looking extremely fragile. The rest of us are all new-found best friends, even if we can't remember each other's names.

This is a final part of the story which I hadn't understood until now. I'd imagined everyone going through their internal ordeals, and wondered how on earth that would make the Church feel like a group. But the power of the shared experience, after it's passed, is remarkable. Everyone swears they're coming back next time.

All religions, in this sense, serve two functions. First, they offer their individual members a path to the divine. Second, they offer a social structure (the meaning of the word religion, 'binding'). For many people, probably most, the social function is more important than the transcendental. Perhaps, when the group becomes more important than the revelation, that's when the priesthood becomes more important than the drug.

I give a lift back to a young man called Andrew, who only a couple of hours before had been throwing up in a bucket by my knee. It was his first big psychedelic experience, and he found it something of an ordeal. (It also turns out he had a large curry the night before.) He's not sure if he learnt anything, not sure how he'll feel about it in a few days. Right now, he's just glad it's over. Away from the group, he confides that he doesn't think he'll be back for more.

6

THE DEVIL'S JUNIPER

After Aref's discoveries about *harmal* use among the Negev Bedouin, I carry on looking with renewed interest for any further indications that it's still used as an intoxicant in the areas where it grows. Sure enough, there are several scattered, mostly anecdotal reports. In Morocco, as I suspected when I bought my seeds there, its psychoactive use is known. The seeds are burnt and the smoke inhaled, both as a medicine to clear the mind and heal headaches and also as a dream-enhancer to make the user clairvoyant and offer protection against the evil eye. In West Pakistan, the seeds are brewed and drunk as a 'narcotic,' whose chemical action is assessed by the botanist author as *"stimulation of the motor tracts of the cerebrum."*

I also find a botanical report on the local use of plants in Ladakh, the high desert region of Himalayan India which borders Tibet, China and Pakistan. Here, apparently, *harmal*

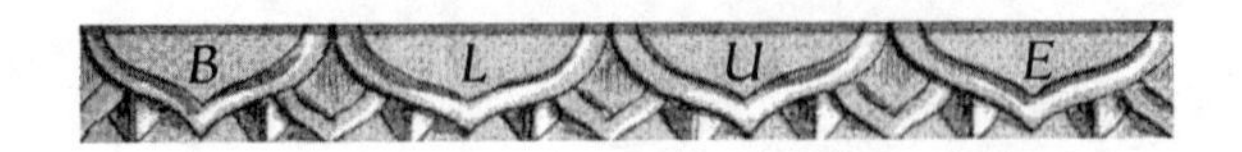

seeds are roasted on a hot iron plate, then pulverised and sieved; the resulting powder is either suspended in milk and drunk, or mixed with tobacco and smoked.

This process, of course, is very familiar. I'm delighted though not entirely surprised to find that my hit-and-miss attempts at extraction and consumption are paralleled so closely on the other side of the world.

The other thing which is particularly interesting about Ladakh is that the River Indus runs through its high mountain gorges. It is, in fact, the land of the *sushoma,* the *soma* mountains of the old Vedic tradition.

I track down a few anthropologists and botanists who've worked in Ladakh, and ask them if they know anything about the distribution of *harmal,* or its local use up on the high plateau. The reference books show that *Peganum Harmala* does indeed grow in Ladakh, at heights of 300-2400 metres around the Indus Valley.

As far as its local use goes, nobody seems to know for sure. Ladakh is too dry to have the varied flora of the rest of India, but the local use of plants and herbs is varied indeed. Much of Ladakh is Buddhist, with various Tibetan and Tantric schools, most of them highly coloured by so-called Bon shamanism, a loose-knit body of folk and magical practices which have survived from the ancient animist system which was there when Buddhism arrived. All these systems coexist with some Hindus, large numbers of Muslims to the west, and the nomadic, yak-herding Changpas. And all of them have highly-evolved systems of plant use in healing and religious ritual.

Eventually I speak to Tim, who's not only spent a long time working out in Ladakh but also has a keen interest in plant psychedelics. He's most interested when I mention *harmal:* he's only recently discovered that it's psychoactive, and is keen to find out more. He tells me that it does indeed grow up and down the Indus, and reels off several spots where it covers the high, bare steppeland.

He's old friends with a man called Amchi, a Tibetan doctor out in Ladakh who also happens to be an expert on local plants and their medicinal uses. He knows that Amchi doesn't use *harmal* in his healing work, because he asked. But Amchi told him the local name for *harmal*. It's known as deshugpa — "the Devil's Juniper."

This is a denser conjunction of *harmal* and *soma* lore than I'd ever imagined. The urge sneaks up on me to find out more about the use of *harmal* in one of the most complex and ancient plant-drug systems in the Old World — and, at the same time, to visit the region where *soma* is supposed to have grown, and from where it was 'lost'.

I think hard about this. I've probably found out as much as I possibly can without going there. Ladakh is a long way away, and I have very little to go on — certainly less than some other places my search has thrown up. It would probably be extremely interesting to go to Konya, even though the Kizilbas are unlikely to talk about their religious practices even with a fluent Turkish speaker, which I'm not. There are many things I'm dying to find out about the Negev Bedouin, but it seems to have taken years for even Aref — himself a Bedouin by birth — to win their trust enough to discuss their *harmal* use even partially. I'm an amateur on a budget. But such a great deal has come to my doorstep, and every time I've made an effort of discovery so far I've been more than generously rewarded. I book a flight to Delhi.

☆ ☆

In the Brahminic tradition, *soma* used to grow in Hemakutu, a land of high mountains on the north side of the Indus River. Here, Indra protected it from legions of *asuras* — devils — who were constantly trying to destroy it. *Soma*'s most common epithet was *parvatavedh* — meaning 'mountain-grown', but also 'elevated' in a more spiritual sense. The highest, most rarefied level of reality was known as *paravata,* a region of the universe in which only the purest essence of life — *soma* — can live.

Ladakh is technically part of Kashmir and India, but is separated from it by a succession of high mountain ranges. From the Indian foothills the Himalayas rise up to nearly 20,000 feet; behind the Himalayas, the Zanskar and Ladakh ranges sweep down from the north-west, isolating a few tiny valley populations for most of the year as the snow makes the high passes impenetrable. Beyond the Ladakh range, the Indus carves out a valley across the beginnings of the Tibetan Plateau, where the altitude drops to a mere 10,000 feet. This is the heart of Ladakh, where the Indus — at this height, still no more than a bubbling, snow-fed stream — affords irrigation and cultivation across its glacial valley. To the east, the Pangong Lake crosses over into occupied Tibet; to the north, the fertile Nubra ("green") Valley leads up to China proper; to the west, the Indus courses through higher and higher gorges towards the Karakoram range and Pakistan.

Flying from Delhi, the flat, featureless plains of India are suddenly replaced by huge moon-mountains which seem almost to scrape the undercarriage, and are dotted with bright blue-green lakes and tarns. Eventually, the first tiny, irrigated valleys appear between them; the plane hardly seems to descend before the white peaks are above us and we bump onto an almost-invisble runway between them.

The sun is hot, the air is cold and thin and, after the hundred-per-cent humidity of Delhi, bone-dry. All the rain falls as snow on the high mountains, leaving Ladakh almost as dry as the Sahara. A few soldiers wander round the airport, creased, weather-beaten faces with high Mongolian cheekbones and wearing thick wool jackets and hats. Buddhist prayer-flags flutter from the scattered barracks and small terminal building.

The bus grinds up the few miles to Leh, the main town, for centuries an important trading post on the Silk Route where

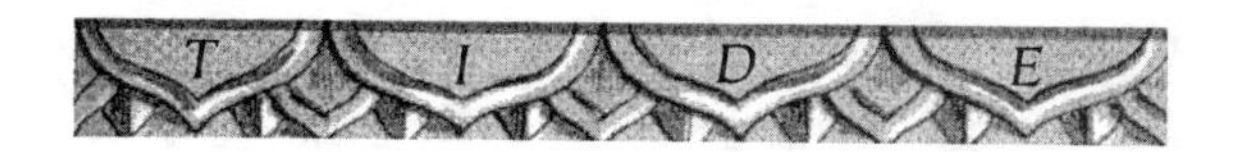

yak trains would set out across the high passes to Bukhara and Samarkand. The road runs along rushing streams and fruit trees; monks in burgundy robes hop on and off among the women in tall, embroidered stove-pipe hats and pointy felt shoes.

I check into a guest-house in an outlying village run by Tim's friend Sonam, and we drink tea. He's a mine of information: climate, geology, trekking routes. He tells me that this is the perfect time to visit: from October until May, Ladakh is cut off by heavy snow, the rivers freeze and the temperature drops to twenty below, making it one of the coldest inhabited places on earth. Now we're seeing the natural snowline, on the peaks of the ranges which surround Leh on every side. He has an expedition he wants to do before the snows come back — he's found an ancient Shiva lingam in a cave some twenty miles from the nearest road, and he wants to find a photographer to take up there to show it to the world, maybe turn it into a pilgrimage site. It's good to find other people on missions no less obscure than my own.

I'm hit by altitude and fatigue, and spend the afternoon in dizzy, light-headed semi-consciousness, feeling like some tiny-lunged creature getting used to the thin atmosphere of an alien planet. I wake with a parched mouth, as if I've been sleeping in front of an air-con vent. Towards evening I wander up to the rocky hill above the village, where the falling sun is reflecting off the dazzling gold spire of a whitewashed *stupa,* or Buddhist shrine.

I make about fifty of the steep steps before a sensation like cold bolts of electricity stabs through my legs — oxygen starvation to the muscles — and I sit down abruptly. The rocky slopes around me are sparsely dotted with weeds and shrubs: small yellow-flowering bushes, shrubs which look like local variants of thyme and heather......and, right beside me, a huge clump of *harmal*.

It's the first time I've ever seen the plant growing, but it's unmistakeable. To be sure, I inch across the scree slope and

crack open a seed-pod. The familiar triangular seeds pop out. I crunch one in my teeth and the opiate bitterness floods through my parched mouth. I squirm onto the rocks beside it and take a few botanical close-up photos, probably looking oddly like I'm grovelling in obeisance to what's almost certainly regarded in these parts as a common weed.

I'm surprised to find it so easily: if it grows here, it probably grows just about everywhere. According to Gordon Hillman, it would probably have established itself here in late Pleistocene times, as the Ice Age receded and the former forests of Central Asia first became steppe-land, thousands of years even before the Vedic culture developed.

I take a sprig back to Sonam, and ask him if this is what's known as *deshugpa*. Either he mis-hears me or he's not familiar with the term: he tells me that's not *shugpa,* it's just a weed. But he has some *shugpa* to show me. We wander round the back to where he has a couple of wheelbarrows full of juniper branches, with their distinctive indigo berries. This is *shugpa*: all the way from Zanskar. It's the most important purifying plant in the local Buddhist culture: Sonam's wife burns it every morning, and they put bunches of the twigs, like witch's hats, on each corner of the roof to protect the house. It's hard to find these days, but Sonam reckons that, a thousand years ago, Ladakh must have been covered with it. Some of the oldest monasteries have ceiling-beams of juniper wood dating back that far.

For the people of Ladakh, the history of their country is the history of Buddhism. The Vedic culture which existed a thousand years before Buddha is prehistory, with no chain of transmission leading down to the present. The Vedic people built in mud brick, and left no remains; the oldest inscription found in these parts is in the Sanskrit Brahmi script, but only dates from around 200BC.

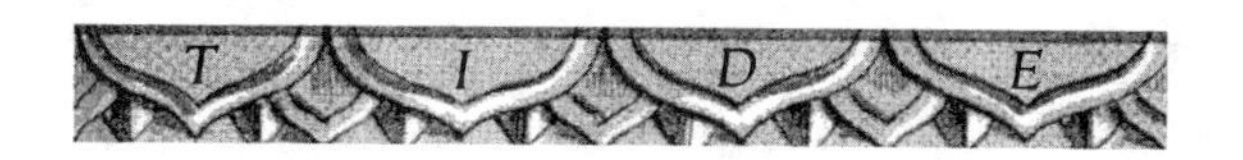

At some point in this prehistory — we can guess, perhaps, around 1000BC — the 'Golden Age' of Vedic culture came to an end, in the time of change in culture and trade which seems to have brought the ancient Bronze Age system of Asia to collapse. The early Hindu tradition which emerged afterwards, of which we know a great deal more, was radically different. First, the centre of activity has left the high Indus Valley and re-established itself down the other great river which drains the Himalayas to the south, the Ganges and its lowland plains. Second, the society which emerges is rigidly stratified and regulated, controlled by he theocratic priest-class of the Brahmins.

And third, *soma* has been 'lost'. But it's not as if all reference to *soma* disappears from the religious literature — quite the opposite, in fact. One of the central roles of the Brahmins is to conduct the rituals and sacrifices which now surround the *soma* sacrament. The *Brahmanas,* the sacred texts of the Brahmin priesthood, are full of instructions and procedures for the *soma* rites. But the *soma* which is used is referred to as *manduka parni* — 'substitute' *soma,* not the original.

Despite the fact that there's no longer any *soma,* its substitutes are surrounded by fiendishly bureaucratic rules. They're sourced from various plants, which are listed in a specific order of preference. First, the reddish-brown *phalguna* plant — perhaps because of its similarity in colour to the original *soma* — but on no account the bright red variety of the same species. If this is unavailable, the *syenahrta* plant may be used instead. Failing this, the *adara* plant; failing that, the *darva* grass or, as a last resort, yellow *kusa* grass. *Kusa* grass, though, is a very poor substitute, and anyone using it must also offer a cow by way of apology.

Since it's plain from the Vedas that the point of drinking *soma* is the intoxication it produces, it seems at first sight astonishing that a non-intoxicating *soma* substitute should even be worth bothering with. But the new *soma* rites are clearly of

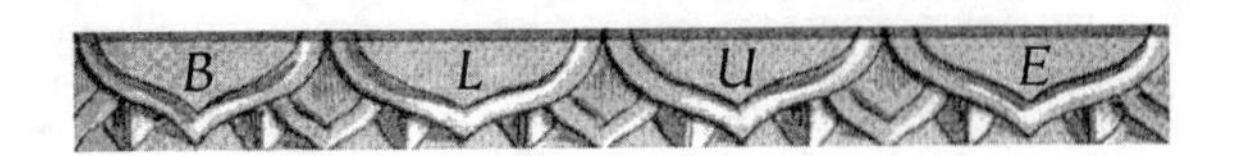

great importance for priests and people alike. The most important initiation for the young priests is their preparation for the *soma* rite, in which they're sprinkled with water and don a cowl and black antelope skin. And, for the people, the right to participate in the *soma* rite is severely means-tested: a man can only drink it if he can show that he has enough saved away to support all his dependents for three years.

Furthermore, *soma* now has to be bought, a procedure which is attended with almost comical degrees of ritual. It can only be bought from the nomadic 'mountain men' who subsist outside the caste system, and the purchase must follow ritualised, almost proto-masonic formulaic exchanges (*"Soma-seller, will you sell King Soma?" "I will sell it"* — etc. etc.). Furthermore, it can only be bought by certain people, on the basis of their lineage. In fact, the rules and prescriptions surrounding the substitute-*soma* ritual are one of the major planks, along with animal sacrifice, in the emergence of the caste system, in which the Brahmins occupy the elevated priest-caste and the rest of the people are divided into soldiers and administrators (*Kshatriyas*), traders and farmers (*Vaisyas*), manual workers (*Sudras*) and the 'untouchables' — *Dalits* — who fall off the end of the scale.

It's still hard to understand why the *soma* ritual was used for this purpose — especially since it involved abandoning the whole point of the ritual in the process. But there's no doubt that the answer lies in the antiquity of the *soma* cult, and the way in which *soma*-drinking came progressively to be read as the marker of an ancient aristocracy. The beginning of the *soma*-pressing ritual is lost in the shared Indo-Iranian antiquity — the same gods, such as Vivasat, preside over it in both the Indian and Iranian traditions. In the earliest days, it was the gods themselves who pressed the *soma*, thereafter the heroic 'god-men' of whom Indra was the commanding representation. As the *soma*-pressing became the role of men, so it became an honour to have *soma*-drinkers among one's ancestors. Coming

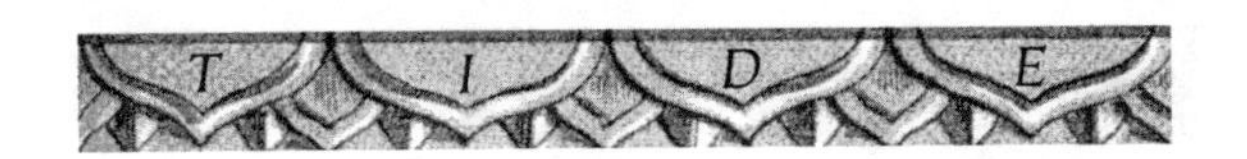

from a long line of *soma*-drinkers went from being a frequent boast in the Vedic hymns to becoming a prerequisite to being allowed to partake in its commemorative sacrifice, where the Brahmins would ask you to give the name of your father, grandfather and great-grandfather.

The Brahmanas are full of prohibitions, but among the most significant is the prohibition of *sura* — alcohol and fermented drinks, which is effectively a prohibition against intoxication of any kind. *Sura*, which is wretched and evil, is frequently compared against *soma*, which is sublime — only, of course, there isn't any *soma*.

It is, however, not forgotten that there was an original *soma*, and that it was a genuine elixir of the gods. In the later Brahminic and ayurvedic texts, this becomes progressively more and more mythologised. The *Sushrut Samhita*, a classic text of early ayurvedic medicine, tells us that the original *soma* was a creeper created by Brahma. Like the mythical plant of immortality in *The Epic of Gilgamesh*, there was only one specimen; as in Gilgamesh, too, it confers immortality on anyone who takes it.

The procedure for taking it is described in detail. The subject must vomit, cleanse himself, fast, pray, extract the juice of the plant, eat a light meal, touch a cow and recite more prayers. After digesting the *soma*, he will vomit again, and the vomit will contain blood and worms. In the evening, he must boil milk and drink it. More worms will emerge and in three days the body will be purged. By the seventh day, all the flesh will have fallen off his bones and he will be a mere skeleton, kept alive by the *soma*. Over the next two weeks his flesh, hair, nails and teeth will grow back. Now he can eat rice and milk; he can expose himself to the sun but — in an odd resonance with the lore of the similarly immortal vampire — not to a mirror. His new body will sustain him for a thousand years.

Presumably if anyone ever turns up a plant with these effects we can safely say that the search for *soma* is over.

Perhaps more instructive, though, is the comparison with elixirs of immortality in other cultures. A sixteenth-century account of the philosopher's stone of the alchemists, for example, is strikingly similar: a French apothecary is said to have produced a powder which sent its subject into a high fever, after which their hair, nails and teeth drop out and regrow. After this, food becomes unnecessary, and all bodily elimination takes place through the sweat glands. The subject is now a higher Adept, and of course immortal.

Similar traditions have also accreted around the *manna* of the Hebrew tradition, as well as various forms of the vampire myth. In each case, they are perhaps best read as legends or metaphors, taking that which is imaginable but unattainable — of which immortality stands as the prime example — and clothing it in an ancient tradition. In the case of *soma*, it's hard to imagine that this could be credible unless the active, intoxicating *soma* was by this stage no more than a dim memory.

In the Brahmin tradition, Indra eventually lost the battle against the *asura* demons to protect his *soma* plantation in Hemakutu, in the Indus Valley. The demons destroyed the *soma* and, with the help of Varuna, begin preparing the local plants into an intoxicating drink — *sura* — the evil effects of which become the curse of mankind.

I begin asking around Leh to see if I can find Amchi, and soon discover that Amchi isn't actually a person at all. An Amchi is a local traditional doctor, practising the Tibetan system of medicine. This has ancient Buddhist roots in texts like the eighth-century *Four Secret Oral Tantras on the Eight Branches of the Essence of Nectar*, and is a broadly holistic system which locates the causes of disease in various imbalances in the elements. Its most well-known practice is the use of pulse measurement as its major diagnostic tool, though there's also a great deal of chat and interrogation which shades into areas analogous to Western psychoanalysis. Medicine is dispensed in the form of specially-made round pills composed of various complexes of local plant extracts and prescribed for diagnoses like blood purification, digestion or nervous disorder. These pills are interesting in that they're presented as quasi-magical items: they're hand-polished, individually wrapped in cloth or even silk, and sealed with wax covered in symbols.

Most Amchis have a pretty good knowledge of local medicinal plants, but it's not hard to discover the name of the one I'm looking for. His name is Amchi Tsewang Smanla, and he has quite a reputation as Ladakh's foremost authority on local ethnobotany. However, he's nowhere to be found at the moment. Apparently he was in Leh but has now gone up country, either trekking or to his house further down the Indus towards Pakistan. General consensus seems to be that he'll be back in a few days.

In the meantime, I decide to travel up the Indus to visit Hemis monastery. This is partly because it sounds similar to Hemakutu, but mostly because it's one of the oldest and most richly-appointed monasteries — effectively the Mecca of Ladakhi Buddhism, since every Ladakhi is supposed to visit it once in their life.

The degree to which Buddhism permeates every aspect of Ladakhi life is something which I've never experienced before. Prayer flags on the corner of every building deliver their prayer up to heaven with every flutter; prayer wheels are mounted in every street, with a metal tongue which clangs a bell every time they turn, and most people deviate from their path to give the drum a couple of spins, filling the air which a constant tinging reminiscent of a more democratised version of English country church bells. (Along with this the constant aural background also includes hawking and spitting, a favourite Ladakhi and Tibetan practice, and the fighting and barking of stray dogs.)

But this constant background of prayer is merely an adjunct to the professional and full-time generation of celestial vibrations which takes place at the monasteries. It's hard to avoid the metaphor of a national electric grid, where prayers are current and the monasteries are the giant batteries and transmitters which store and send it. The monastery system as it now stands was set up by the 17th-century King Deldan, who found himself in dire need of psychic protection against the expansionist Tibetans. He conscripted the second sons of every available family into all the monasteries until he had a full staff of 108 lamas at each, which he had calculated would be necessary to generate the requisite one hundred million *om mani padme hum's* a year which he reckoned would keep him safe.

But, along with the industrial-scale rosary which this represents, the monasteries also function as a theocratic priest-craft which is probably still closer to Zoroaster's society than it is to the rest of the modern world. Dealing with sparse agricultural resources and such long winters, the mainstay of the Ladakhi economy has always been the cooperative, and any surplus has traditionally been stored, along with the chants and *mantras,* at the monasteries. As such, they were — and partly still are — government, bank and church combined. And, historically, Hemis has always been the Bank of England and Westminster Abbey: the monastery where the king's younger son was traditionally sent, and where the largest assemblies of the monasteries took place.

I'm at the bus station shortly after dawn, trying to locate a bus which will take me there. As near as I can work out, there's a bus there but no bus back. Another Westerner catches my eye, who I can tell straight away is English. He looks about seventy, and very like William Burroughs, except that he's missing more teeth and is even more shabbily-dressed, with a floppy knitted cap perched like an undersize tea-cosy on his head and hands scabbed and veined with heavy sunburn. He's jabbering away in Hindi, which none of the Ladakhis understand. I immediately decide that he's one of the coolest people I've ever clapped eyes on, and try to find out what he's up to. Apparently he's trying to get to Stok, a nearby palace, but the bus seems to have left half an hour early. I pitch him the idea of Hemis, and he decides to come along too. I tell him that the snag is that there's no bus back. Never mind, he says cheerfully, I'm sure we'll have an adventure.

As glimpsed between armpits, hats and chickens on the overcrowded bus, the Indus is an unbelievably bright green, glacial melt running over smooth white stones. Age-old irrigation spreads the barley fields across its plain and halfway up its slopes. Mud-bricks made of its compacted silt dry in the sun, still the same regulation size as those which built the first Indus cities of Harappa and Mohenjo-Daro centuries before the Vedas. Cattle roam unpenned across the valley, the river, the road. Outside the bus, much is as it must have been four thousand years ago.

Frank, my elderly companion, turns out to be great company. He originally came to these parts in 1947, where he served in the British army in the last days before Partition and Independence. Now he's back travelling on his pension, which his wife sends out to him on the promise that he won't go to war-torn Srinagar and that he'll be back for the family Christmas. He's been out here for weeks, living on around three pounds a day, travelling third-class on the trains and sleeping in the cheapest flophouses. His good humour is irrepressible, light years from the complaints about rip-offs which most younger travellers seems to use as the common coin of conversation. He won't say anything bad about anywhere or anyone, until I ask him about his stay in Calcutta, when he leans across confidentially and describes the city as "a bit run down, actually."

The bus crosses the Indus on a narrow wrought-iron bridge and grinds its way up into the mountains, past terraced fields of barley and innumerable *stupas,* shrines and crumbling domes. The monastery perches high among the lichen-stained rocks, the peak of the mountain at its back. It consists of a courtyard lined with dozens of prayer-wheels, off which a

series of faded frescoed doorways lead to prayer-rooms, sleeping quarters and the central shrine. This is dominated by a giant orange-robed Buddha smeared with accretions of gold leaf, monks busying themselves with its feeding and watering or else working through their *mantras* on the prayer-mats around it. One side of the shrine is shelved, and houses the library: hundreds of volumes of hand-written parchments, loose-leaved and wrapped in tasselled silk, the many sacred books of Tibetan Buddhism translated from Sanskrit, Tibetan and Hindi and back again.

One of the frescoes in the porch interests me particularly. It's a huge mandala depicting various stages on the wheel of life: at the top, the realm of heaven, a crowded canvas presided over by a celestial Buddha, at the bottom a hell like something out of Dante or Bosch, a mass of bloated, deformed figures breathing fire and transforming into beasts. This is surrounded by an enormous cartoon-like demonic entity who holds the wheel in front of him, his clawed feet and hands projecting outside its perimeter. His head projects from the top, his fanged incisors gripping the wheel. In the centre of his forehead his third eye is open, and around his forehead runs a crown of skulls.

I ask one of the monks about it, and piece together an explanation from broken English and gestures. This is a Buddha who has opened his third eye, so that he can hold all the world, good and evil, in his arms. This is a path of power, will and desire, which makes it a high-risk strategy. The crown of skulls symbolises the danger of his enterprise.

Emerging from the monastery, I only have to wander a few yards through the ruined *stupas* before I find my own key to the opening of the third eye. *Harmal* is growing everywhere; up here, it's still in flower, small yellow and white blossoms dotted across the landscape.

It seems very unlikely that it has any use in local Buddhist culture, which has done nothing if not cultivate nonchemical alternatives to the kind of state which *harmal* induces. Already, I've noticed that the drug culture here, such as it is, seems to revolve almost entirely round alcohol, which is drunk in the form of *chang*, a sour barley beer very much in evidence around the harvest festivals. I hear it's possible to get hold of opium still in Leh, though not, I imagine, for Westerners; I hear, too, that down in Dharamsala, the headquarters of the Tibetan government in exile and home of the Dalai Lama, some of the younger Tibetans are beginning to discover opium and heroin, the predictable flip-side of an alcohol culture. But the Ladakhis seem to have little appetite for the revved-up, intensified consciousness of stimulants or psychedelics; the basic orientation of their culture seems to be in disengaging from this level of the mental process, for which the occasional use of alcohol is highly suitable.

As advertised, there's no bus back from Hemis, and Frank and I find ourselves walking back down to the Indus past the barley-harvesters, men and women, who sing to each other in call-and-response refrains as they work. Halfway down the valley is a huge wall of loose stones, about twenty feet across and at least half a mile long; as we pass it, we realise that every stone is elaborately carved with a prayer in Tibetan script.

We walk for miles down the Indus, pausing to help a monk repair a puncture on his scooter, eventually getting a local ride and being dropped off near another monastery. We cross the Indus again, this time on a narrow rope-bridge hung with tattered prayer-flags, and make another mountain ascent. This *gompa*, as monasteries are called, is quieter than Hemis: we approach, enter and pad around quietly for several minutes before one solitary monk approaches us. I ask him if I can go up onto the roof, and he comes with me.

The Indus Valley is several miles wide at this point, terraced fields receding into the blasted lunar mountain range beyond. On the edge of the *gompa* roof is a huge bunch of juniper stalks bristling up into the sky; beside it, rather incongruously, is a solar panel. *Shugpa,* I point out. His expansive gesture seems to include both the juniper and the solar panel. "*Gompa* protector," he pronounces in scrupulous English.

The sun's setting as we leave the monastery, and by the time we reach the road the cold night wind is sweeping in off the desert and the villagers are gathering round kerosene stoves and kneading barley dough. We walk for miles again, picking up a couple of local rides and eventually come bearing in to Leh on the back of an army truck at around midnight. Frank leaps over the side of the truck and profers a bag of fruit to the soldiers in the rig.

Well, he says as we separate in the pitch darkness, it certainly was an adventure.

☆ ☆

In 1936 Antonin Artaud, theatrical innovator, opiate addict and eventual lunatic, went to Central America to take peyote cactus with the Tarahumara Indians. For the rest of his life, he maintained that the few days he spent in this peyote ritual were the only ones where he was at peace with himself, and where life made sense.

He also developed an obsession with a particular shade of the colour blue, which stared back at him constantly from above the peaks of the Sierra Madre. He decided it was exactly the same shade of blue that the pre-Renaissance Italian painters had used in the skies above their landscapes. He intuited from this that these pre-Renaissance painters had all been initiated into a secret science which we haven't yet rediscovered. In an odd parallel to my search for the blue tide, he also claimed that the original transmitters of this secret science had been the Persian Magi.

One of the unexpected themes among the people I meet in Ladakh turns out to be the obsessive pursuit of a particular shade of the colour blue. One young Indian has just returned from Pangong Lake, which he tells me is a colour he's never seen before ("You know copper sulphate crystals? Well, after this lake, they look grey"). Another is determined to photograph the night sky just before the moon rises, when it's "blue like the Arabian Nights". I'm reminded of the psychologist Oliver Sacks and his pursuit of a particular shade of indigo which he saw a couple of times as a young man after smoking cannabis. I can't remember people becoming similarly interested in particular shades of red, or green, or yellow. I wonder what it is about blue.

Meanwhile I'm still searching for Amchi. There's still no sign of him in Leh, so I decide to journey down the Indus to find him.

The road west is a single track of well-maintained tarmac which cuts through the high moonscape desert before joining the Indus at the point where the Zanskar river, flowing through from the mountain range to the south, joins it. The Zanskar is churning with mud and silt, and the confluence of the two rivers shows a clean demarcation between the bright green of the Indus and the Zanskar's frothy brown. From here on the Indus becomes a muddy torrent, cutting its way deeper into the rock and forming dark gorges which the sun only penetrates for a few hours a day.

Most of the sparse traffic is army convoys, and militarised checkpoints begin to appear with more frequency as we approach the Pakistan border. I hitch a ride with three generations of an extended Kashmiri family: the father is on his way to some unspecified "official business" near the border. I'm dropped off at Amchi's village, where I'm pointed in the direction of a large house across a couple of now-bare barley fields. One of his daughters invites me up into the main room of the house, an open hearth/kitchen with a huge silver- and brass-decorated woodburning stove. I take a seat on a low bench beside a couple of Ladakhi men who are drinking churned, salty gug-gur tea and tipping barley flour into the

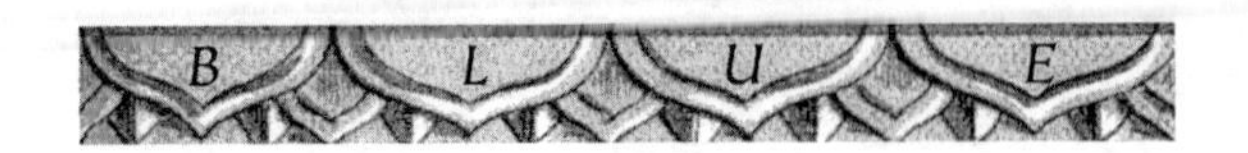

dregs to make spongy flour-and-tea patties. Amchi's wife and daughters produce an enormous number of beautiful brass pots and pans and make chapatis and vegetables. After a substantial and good-humoured lunch I eventually establish that Amchi isn't here — in fact, he's in Leh. I leave with his address.

That night I end up in a small village in the mountains above the Indus. The nights are getting cold, almost down to zero, but I curl up in a blanket on the roof to wait for the only firm date I've had in my diary since I arrived: a total eclipse of the full moon.

The moon, of course, is Soma: the sun is Agni, and the constant struggles and marriages of the two heavenly bodies reflect the symbiosis of the principles of Agni and Soma on the earth below. In the winter, Soma overpowers Agni, and the scorching heat and drought of Agni's summer reign is counterbalanced by the earth's self-enveloping pregnancy which will bear fruit when Agni returns. The moon is a constant Vedic metaphor for *soma*: the brew is often compared to it in fullness and whiteness, the stages of its preparation to the moon's waxing and waning.

The night sky at this altitude and level of dryness is dazzling. The first couple of nights, I stared at it for several minutes without being able to extract a single constellation from the mass of stars. Eventually I found Cassiopeia, so buried in other unfamiliar constellations that even its distinctive W-shape had to be more or less guessed at. Prominent every night has been another entirely unfamiliar constellation in the shape of a perfect spiral. One night I saw a huge meteorite seem to explode over Leh, and scatter its sparks across the town like a dying firework; in Ladakhi, these are known as "broken stars".

The eclipse has, like all eclipses, a timeless quality. I'm conscious in the minutes of its stasis of the Himalayas as they were: *devbhumi,* the abode of the gods, immutable home of Soma and Indra.

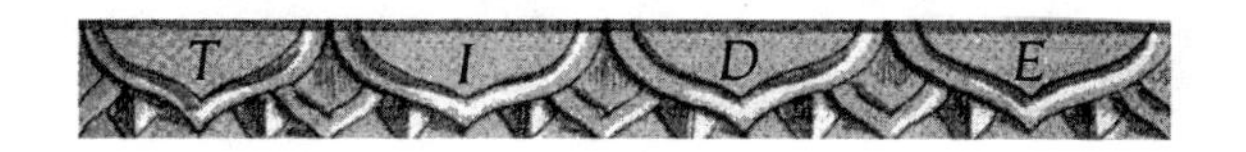

☆ ☆

Back in Leh, I locate Amchi's address: a small outbuilding in the grounds of a rambling guesthouse. My knock is answered by a couple of young children from whom I establish that the man is out on his rounds. I climb another peak to watch the sunset over the town, and find an Indian gentleman with a spectacular handlebar moustache setting up an elaborate double exposure with an array of cameras, lenses, tripods and filters. He turns out to be a major in the Bombay Rifles whose 'hobby' is photographing inaccessible Himalayan vistas. He seems to have been everywhere, and I plug him for information. In turn, once he discovers that I have some experience with film, he solicits my opinion on "artistic" questions of lighting and exposure.

I ask him about the country towards the Pakistan border, and the people who live there. He tells me that they're known locally as Drugpas, and that they're quite different from the rest of the Ladakhis. I've heard they're mostly Muslims; he tells me that some of them are Muslims, some Buddhists, but neither of these bear much relation to the Islam or Buddhism which surrounds them. They're simply different people. I ask him in what way. Well, he tells me, they're the last surviving Aryans.

'Aryans' is a term which can't really be used without a frisson in the West these days, though Indians still use it freely and without embarrassment. The terms 'Aryan' and 'Indo-European' were used more or less interchangeably from the last century through to the 1930s; now, of course, 'Indo-European' has become the standard, though no-one seems quite sure any more of exactly what it means. I ask him exactly what he means by 'the last Aryans'.

You know, he tells me, the people who were here before Buddhism. The first Indians. The Vedic people. Some of them stayed up here in the mountains. The Drugpas are their

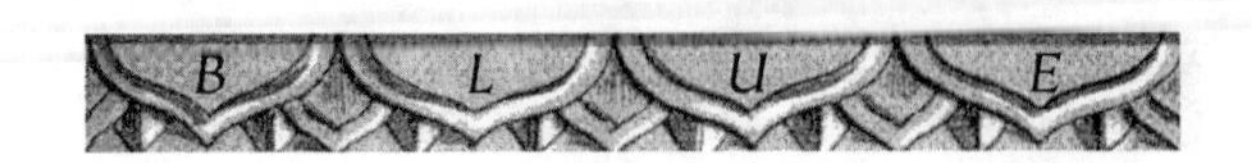

descendents. I ask him how he knows that these people are the Vedic 'Aryans'. Well, he tells me, their language is very ancient, still quite like Sanskrit. And they're very light-skinned. They look almost European. But it's hard to find out much about them. They're not unfriendly exactly, but their language is very difficult and they're suspicious of people prying into their culture. They wear similar clothes to other Ladakhis — felt hats, wooly jerkins, jewellery — but with some particular differences. Their most noticeable custom is that they wear flowers in their hair. It's hard to find out exactly what this means, but basically whenever they pass a sacred spot, somewhere of special significance, they'll either lay down a flower from their heads, or pick a new one, or both. Also, they're much more scrupulous than other Indians about the ritual prohibition of cattle. They won't eat beef, of course, but they also won't even drink cow's milk. Occasionally they do keep cows, but only to cross-breed with yak and produce sturdy, lower-altitude beasts of burden called *dzos*.

'Drugpa', it turns out, is simply the Tibetan for 'herdsman'; it's hard to find any local confirmation of the Drugpas' relation to the Vedic people as there's so little in the way of ancient history of Ladakh. But their language should furnish some proof of kinship, if there is any. Since the linguistic work of Sir William Jones, the tree of 'Indo-European' languages has been frequently constructed and re-constructed, to attempt to follow its root back to the notional source of the first Indo-Europeans. The homeland of these nebulous ancestors, however, hasn't yielded to linguistic analysis: competing theories have located it anywhere from Turkey to the Balkans to the Caspian. Recently, it's become clear that these notional Indo-Europeans will probably always be impossible to identify among the vast range of prehistoric peoples and the sporadic appearances of agriculture, wheeled chariots, sun-worship and other supposed markers of future Indo-European domination.

It's also become clear that the similarity of languages

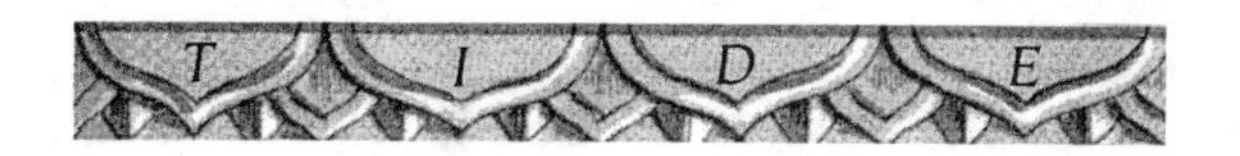

between the various Indo-European peoples didn't bring with it any particular sense of kinship. The Greeks called the Indians *barbaros* while the Indians called the Greeks *barbaras,* neither of them recognising that the similarity between their languages formed any kind of bond. So the Drugpas' language wouldn't necessarily tell us much about any culture they might have shared with the Vedic people — but it might be a start.

Although there's no ancient history in Ladakh, the ancient history of the West does speak vaguely of the upper Indus Valley and the people before the Buddhists. The area is first mentioned in Western chronicles by Herodotus, our source for the story of the Scythians and their cannabis-smoke tents. But what he has to say about the Indus doesn't quite carry the same immediate ring of truth. He tells us that the Indians who live there are savage and warlike, and very wealthy on account of the gold which is to be found in the sandy desert surrounding the mountains. In this desert lives a particular species of ant which is larger than a fox but smaller than a dog; these ants dig burrows and throw up mounds of gold. The Indians wait until the heat of the day, when the ants are deep underground, then arrive on camels, fill up their bags with the ants' gold-dust and ride away as quickly as possible: once the ants have worked out what's happening they come racing out of their burrows in hot pursuit.

This story is perhaps not quite so bereft of truth as it initially seems. Other sources suggest that the Indus Valley was rich with gold in antiquity, and probably still is. More strikingly, a folklorist at the turn of the last century tried asking local people if they had any stories about gold-digging ants: not only did he collect two long but separate versions of the same myth, but he was actually shown the species of ant in question. It was, of course, considerably smaller than a fox — this part of the story had obviously grown on the journey to Europe — but, more than two thousand years on, this must still count as impressive corroboration for Herodotus. (An alternative face-saving modern reading is that the 'ants' were actually marmots, a large beaver-sized burrowing rodent still common across the Central Asian steppes.)

A day in the local library establishes a few basic facts. The Drugpas are known in Western scholarship as the 'Dards', a name assigned to them by Moorcroft, the first European outside Jesuit missionaries to visit Ladakh, which he did in 1822 on a trade mission on behalf of the East India Company. I establish later that, as I suspected, the people in question have never referred to themselves as 'Dards' any more than the Nizari Isma'ilis called themselves Assassins. They're actually a loosely-related group of various people speaking more than a dozen different languages, as a linguistic survey established in 1906. 'Dard' was an ancient classical name for the Indus Valley people which we know from sources such as Pliny; it was reinforced, perhaps, by the name of the largest Drugpa settlement, Da — which, I recall, was also the name of the *harmal* entities channelled by Skip in his opiated nightmares. The western reaches of the Indus were in fact given the name of 'Dardistan' by Victorian geographers, which still appears on some maps in the mountainous north-east of Pakistan.

The languages of the Drugpas, though, turn out to be very interesting indeed. Not only are they from an ancient Indo-European root, but they can be quite precisely dated. They're from the period before the migration to the Ganges, bearing many similarities to the oldest Indo-European we know; but they have no traces of the Avestan, or Iranian, branch, which split off after the earliest days of the shared Indo-Iranian culture. This locates them quite specifically in the period of the Vedas.

In modern linguistic terms, their languages are at the root of what's known as the 'Indic' group, which includes modern Hindi, Urdu and Bengali and is spoken by over 500 million people across the Indian subcontinent. Outside the subcontinent, the only known Indic language

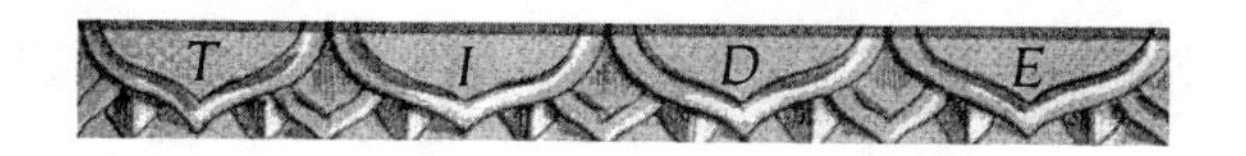

still spoken is Romany, suggesting that Europe's best-known surviving nomads arrived from somewhere in North India during the Middle Ages.

These ancient Indo-European roots mean that the Drugpa languages include many words which are strikingly familiar to Europeans. Water, for example, is *"wasr"*, door is *"dar"*, and other words are extremely close to French: a stick, apparently, is *"baston"*. It's this, combined with their pale skins, which has repeatedly led both Westerners and Ladakhis to proclaim them as some kind of long-lost distant relatives. As the Ladakhis put it, "they have bulging eyes and long noses, just like Europeans". The Jews of Bokhara, apparently, used to consider them honorary members of the Lost Tribes. But the most celebrated explanation, which developed through the nineteenth century, was that they were pockets of descendents of Alexander the Great's army. This explanation was offered for a great variety of Central Asian peoples, and most memorably romanticised by Kipling in *The Man Who Would Be King*. The lingusitic evidence, of course, means that this can't be entirely true, although of course intermarriage may have occurred. But the widespread repetition of the legend across centuries and huge swathes of Asia must, I think, be attributable to something else — probably the perennial surprise of Europeans arriving in the wilds of the Himalayas only to find, unaccountably, that the local savages are surprisingly like themselves.

But, beyond the linguistic evidence, I'm delighted to find that there are also some traces of the Vedic religion among the beliefs of the 'Dards' or Drugpas. Even through the millennia and the conversions to Buddhism (around two thousand years ago) and Islam (little more than a century ago), *"Indr"* is still in their pantheon; though his status has become rather minor, some of their other terms such as 'rainbow' (*"ind'ro"*) and 'earthquake' (*"indr'ist"*) suggest that he must once have played a more all-encompassing role.

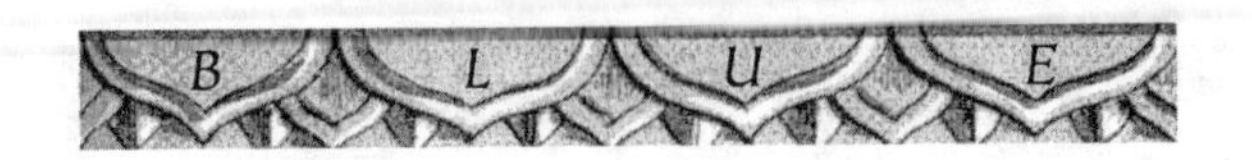

If the Drugpas — or rather, lest we forget, their 4000-year-old ancestors — didn't follow the rest of their people down to the Ganges, they wouldn't have witnessed the social and religious revolution of the Brahmins, including the full ritualisation of the *soma* sacrifice. Instead, we would expect their culture to reflect the practices of cattle-raiding and chariot-racing, and their central ritual from the distant past to have been horse-sacrifice.

The traditional Indic horse-sacrifice, the *asvamedha,* is much-beloved by Indo-European scholars as the defining cultural marker of the notional people whose kinship they're trying to establish. It involved four priests selecting a prize stallion, which would then be allowed to roam free for a year, followed by four hundred warriors who would remove obstacles from its path and make sure that it didn't couple with any mares. After a year, it would be brought back, and would pull the king's chariot while dozens of minor sacrifices were enacted. Then it would be killed, and the king's favourite wife would 'cohabit' with the dead horse under covers, after which it would be dismembered into three parts.

Classicists, archaeologists and ethnologists have of course had an extended field day interpreting this tradition, especially since it compares with other ceremonies far-flung across the 'Indo-European' world: the 'October Equus' sacrifice in Imperial Rome, and the medieval Irish inauguration of the Kings of Ulster. It's been made to stand for the shared traditions of all the Indo-European peoples, for the universal tradition of the symbolic sacrifice of the God-King, and the partition of the horse into three has, in particular, been claimed as a representation of the supposedly distinctive division of Indo-European societies into the three castes of nobles, warriors and peasants which later came to underlie both the caste and feudal systems.

☆ ☆

This week, the social life of Leh is dominated by the finals of the all-Ladakhi polo championship. I've never been to a polo match before, but some Ladakhi friends invite me along, and I'm curious in any case to witness the sport in the country of its origin. (Its origin is actually a little further west, in the Karakorams — Gilgit and Chitral compete for the title of 'home of polo' — and its originators weren't Ladakhis or Tibetans but people more like the Drugpas. When international championships are held the Ladakhis, who tend to use polo tournaments as an excuse to celebrate and drink *chang,* usually lose to their stricter Islamic neighbours to the west.)

The polo ground, Leh's only municipal sporting arena, is packed. Old men, young men, women, monks and a few tourists cram onto the concrete steps surrounding the sand-filled arena. Crumbling *stupas,* huge mountains and the Leh monastery on its beetling crag form an impressive backdrop.

The mounts and riders appear on the pitch, and the game starts without ceremony. This is a polo that takes no prisoners; I'm glad I was warned not to sit in the front row, where the ball frequently comes trickling towards the terrified audience followed by several opposing horses galloping full-tilt towards the edge, surmounted by mallet-wielding competitors obviously blind to any obstruction. Whenever a goal's scored, it's announced by a blast of braying Tibetan horns, a clashing of cymbals and an ominous roll of kettle-drums; at this point, both the teams rush to change ends. Once the team with the ball is in position they can turn and charge at their opponents, ready or not.

It's during this manoeuvre, watching one side descend on the other like a wolf on the fold, that the obvious strikes me between the eyes: polo has its roots in a ritualised form of cattle-raiding. The ball stands as a token for the cattle-herd, which the two teams of horsemen must compete to corral around the field, moving in phalanxes and outflanking their opponents.

The game is over in a breathless and exhilarating forty minutes. The Indian Army team, far better-equipped, wins 3-1.

Asking around later, I discover that there are a few Drugpas living in Leh. I'm taken to meet one, who's a young taxi-driver — the only Drugpa taxi-driver in Ladakh, as most of them live deep in the country and don't speak any English or have urban job skills. As soon as I meet him, I realise that I've seen a few other Drugpas around: they have a distinctive look, with pale skin and dark hair, that wouldn't be out of place anywhere around the Mediterranean. If I'd met them in London, I wouldn't be surprised to hear them speaking with English accents. A Lost Tribe indeed.

That night I meet a Canadian at dinner who brings me closer than ever before to the classic urban myth about the Drug of the Assassins. He's just arrived from Delhi, where one of the first Westerners he met was in a wild-eyed and disorientated state. His tale was that he'd taken a ride in an auto-rickshaw, when a young Indian man had jumped in and offered him a home-made cookie. He'd refused, but the man had eaten one himself and carried on insisting; eventually the young traveller had caved in. The next thing he remembered was waking up three days later, dizzy and feverish, in a hotel room he didn't recognise, with everything stolen including his boots.

It's always unsettling to encounter something which seems to be both a myth in its classic form and something which has genuinely happened to someone. This is textbook datura intoxication, the story which has resonated throughout history from Egypt to Colombia — and yet this sober young man is giving it to me direct from the horse's mouth. But this is probably part of the nature of many urban myths: the truth isn't that they never happen, or indeed that they always happen. It's probably closer to a scenario where they do indeed happen occasionally, but those incidents become amplified and distorted to the extent to which already-existing preconceptions nourish them. This one, I'm sure, will spread far and wide among the travelling community, with its classic themes of the fiendish local drug, the classic scam and the ultimate tourist nightmare. What's more, I'm sure the "including his boots" detail, faithfully relayed to me and an irresistable detail to pass on, will survive many generations of Chinese whispers intact.

Next morning I'm walking through town when I distinctly smell *harmal* burning. I pause; the street is empty apart from a few stray cows and dogs munching last night's rubbish. Eventually I track it down to a Kashmiri shop where the owner is just opening for business. I tell him it's a beautiful smell, and that I recognise it. I ask him what his name is for it. He tells me, "good morning smell". No, I tell him, I mean the seeds that you're burning: what do you call them in Kashmiri? Ah, he replies, yes, we call them "good morning smell".

That evening, around sunset, I return to Amchi's lodgings. Once more the door is opened by two young boys: different ones from last time. But this time, the doctor is in.

Meeting Amchi doesn't entirely disperse the mystery of who he is. Leh is in the middle of its daily power-cut, and we sit down on low stools in almost pitch blackness. The two young boys, aged around six and four, turn out to be his sons, and are quietly asked to make us tea.

For the first time since I've been here, I'm able to be specific about what I'm looking for. I tell Amchi I'm interested in a particular plant. He asks me which one. I tell him it has various names: *harmal...esfant...*he's straight back to me with: "Ah, *Peganum Harmala!*" We settle in with our tea.

It turns out that I'm not the first person to ask him about *harmal* and its psychoactive uses. He had several conversations with Tim about it, and also with a German biologist who showed a particular interest in it.

I ask him about the local name *deshugpa*. Why is it the 'devil's juniper'? He tells me that quite often, in Tibetan and Ladakhi, the 'devil's' epithet is used to identify something which can easily be confused with something else. Like, I suggest, English names like 'fool's gold', or the various fungi which are known as 'false' whatevers. Exactly: the name means, effectively, 'false juniper'.

But, I point out, *harmal* and juniper look nothing like each other. He agrees: it must be because they're used in the same way. Juniper is the most important plant in the daily ritual of Tibetans and Ladakhis: their "good morning smell" and much more besides. It's a plant of purification, both for the air and atmosphere and also given as a purgative medicine. Exactly like *harmal* in the Arab world, I tell him. That must be the meaning of *deshugpa,* he tells me. That it's the plant which is used exactly like *shugpa,* except by the 'other people'.

People like the Drugpas?

People like the Drugpas.

I ask him what its uses are in Amchi medicine. None at all, apparently. It's not part of the complex of plants which is used for preparing the pills. I find it odd that a plant which has so many medicinal uses across Central Asia should be regarded as having no medicinal value in Ladakh. He corrects me: just because they don't use it doesn't mean they regard it as having no medicinal value. In Tibetan medical theory, all plants are medicinal. It's just that some of them we haven't found the correct medical use for yet.

Nonetheless, its absence from Amchi medicine seems to me to be significant. Amchi is a tradition which, along with many of the people who use it, has its roots in the east — Tibet and China. *Harmal,* on the contrary, has its roots in the west — in the Middle East and Central Asia, the same as the people who use it as a daily purifying and ritual plant. Chinese medicine is a very traditional system, and is unlikely to have had *harmal* as an indigenous plant until relatively late in its evolution, by which time the main precepts of its plant medicine would already have been well-established.

It's quite hard in daily life in Ladakh to distinguish between 'ethnic groups': very few of the people look purely Tibetan, and historically almost everyone is descended from the early 'Tibeto-Dard' kingdoms where the people who had their origins in the east and the west mixed, and the tides of Buddhism and then Islam rose and fell across the region. So it's particularly interesting that the separate use of power plants should have survived where the boundaries of religion and race have long since crumbled. Where Buddhist and Muslim, Mongol and 'Aryan' are all relative terms, the line between the juniper users and the *harmal* users has stayed intact.

I ask Amchi if he thinks the Drugpas, for example, still use *harmal* as an intoxicant. He tells me he has no way of knowing. Despite his lifelong interest in local plant use, it's the kind of thing you could live several lifetimes and not find out. Maybe the older men, down the Indus in Dha-Hanu...he'll keep his eyes and ears open.

Of course, the Drugpas are removed by millennia from their Vedic ancestors. Of course, it's highly unlikely that they'll tell me much about their most obvious customs, let alone their most sacred ones. Of course, the literal identification of *harmal* with *soma* isn't really the point of my researches. Nevertheless, the spectre has now been raised: it's theoretically possible that the last Vedic 'Aryans' are still drinking *soma* in the Indus Valley. No matter that the terms 'Vedic', 'Aryan' and '*soma*', strictly speaking, need to be so hedged around with qualifications as to be almost meaningless — the possibility can't be allowed to remain unexplored.

But how to explore it? The Dha-Hanu area is theoretically open to tourists, but it requires a permit which in practice is usually only given to groups of four or more visitors. It's possible to head out and chance it — I've met a traveller who did just that, and got to stay overnight without difficulty. I'd need to stay longer than overnight, of course.

Walking through Leh's main bazaar, I notice a trekking agency advertising Dha-Hanu as one of its destinations. Looking closer, I find the following carefully hand-printed underneath it:

Cultural Tour. See Last Race of Aryans
Confined to Indus Valley.

This notice strikes me by turns as absurd, unbearably sad and strategically promising. I wander in and the man behind the desk sends out for cups of tea.

I ask him what he means, the 'last race of Aryans'. It's hard to get any kind of specific answer to this, since it calls on a prehistory of the region which, in most people's minds, doesn't really exist. He tells me, you know, the last Aryans. I ask him, you mean like the Vedic people? Yes. Have they always been there? Yes. Did they migrate there from the Karakorams? Yes.

I ask him about his cultural tour. He says he's not sure when the next one is leaving. There's not much demand for it. I tell him, perhaps I'd be better off just rustling up some volunteers and getting transport together myself. No, no, he insists. Then you'd miss the cultural tour. I ask him what the cultural tour consists of. He tells me, you eat traditional food. Then the Drugpas do their dance for you. You pay them little little money, you can take photos.

I tell him, thanks for the tea.

☆ ☆

I'm still trying to work out an alternative strategy when I'm overtaken by events.

It's late September, and Ladakh is suddenly moving into its long winter. The barley harvest is in, and the cattle are now unpenned and are wandering the streets of Leh in huge aimless herds. Apparently there are even a few yak who've come down from the mountains. I've picked up many interesting titbits of yak lore, mostly from Sonam. Yak are unbelievably well-insulated: if a yak falls asleep in the snow, the snow beneath it doesn't even melt. Quite often they'll fall asleep in near-freezing rivers, and only wake up several hours later when the cold eventually percolates through. This means, of course, that they're unable to sweat or lose heat, confining them to the high peaks. Their transmigration is a sure sign of winter.

This dramatic seasonal shift is reflected in the life of the town. Restaurants and hotels are closing, boarded up with signs reading "reopening next June".The stalls of Tibetan, Chinese and Indian food are giving way to the winter's staple slop of rice and *dal*. I half-expect a sign to announce: "will the last person to leave please turn out the lights". The airline office is beseiged day and night by crowds of people not even attempting to book a flight, but simply trying to edge their waiting-list numbers down into double figures. Low waiting-list numbers are traded frantically outside the building.

There are only two land routes out of Ladakh. One goes to Srinagar, and barely runs any more due to the tension in Kashmir. The other heads due south down to the hills of Himachal Pradesh, but to do so must traverse two of the world's three highest motorable mountain-passes. The army and government stop maintaining this road around the middle of September, after which it's left to private vehicles and buses to chance it. Everyone buzzes with the latest radio weather reports: snow is already falling on the high passes, and every bus out may be the last.

I can't afford the doubtful luxury of taking my chances on a wait of days, weeks or months in Leh. Reluctantly, I jump on the last bus out.

EPILOGUE: *BLUE TIDE*

The bus ride is an experience to be savoured but not necessarily repeated. We set off before dawn, and for two days we wheeze through bleak mountains and valleys, deserted except for sporadic groups of yak-herding nomads. The mountain ranges run down to the south-east, eventually drawing us away from our destination and forcing us to mount the precarious nests of switchbacks and loops which take us over the high passes, their snows dazzling under bright skies and their desolate summits marked with clusters of prayer-flags. We frequently have to choc the wheels of the bus while the driver negotiates the vertiginous bends; at one point the pass is blocked by an abandoned truck, jacked-up at a forty-five degree angle where the road has sheared away beneath it, and we have to spend several hours rebuilding the road before we can advance.

The bus eventually delivers us to the green, subtropical lowland hills around Manali, which offers another strange conjunction of drugs and religion. Manali is where Manu, the Hindus' sole survivor of the great Flood, was eventually

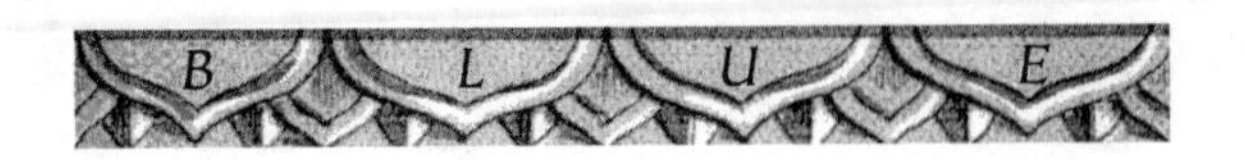

beached, and is sacred to his memory. It's also, especially in the minds of young Westerners, a by-word — virtually a brand-name — for India's finest black hashish.

In crossing the Himalayas, I've also crossed a major watershed in drug cultures. It's cannabis season in the valleys around Manali, and the air is thick with aromatic pollen. The plant grows everywhere: at the roadside, in the hills, at the bus-stops, in a bewildering subspeciation of strains, bushy and spindly, tidy pagoda-shaped stalks and squat, splay-leafed bushes. This is Shiva country, the villages dotted with ancient stone temples where robed, leonine *saddhus* squat clutching cannabis chillum-pipes with serene thousand-yard stares.

In my brief stopover I gather that this area, too, is rife with ancient isolate communities analogous to the Drugpas. In the connecting Parvati Valley, there's a mountain village called Malana which is cut off from the rest of the area for at least half the year. Its five hundred or so inhabitants live outside Indian and state law: no army, police or government officials have ever been allowed to set foot there. Instead, a strict and arcane version of the caste system rules — visitors must wait on the edge of the village for permission to enter, which will be refused if they're wearing any leather. Once inside the village, they are strictly prohibited from touching any of the inhabitants, or certain sacred stones around the temple. Heavy penalties are levied for transgression: for Indians usually a goat, for foreigners a steep cash fine. There's a school in the village, but very few of the population have ever attended. Local justice is meted out by a two-chamber parliament, one chamber from each side of the village, where cases are heard by a jury of the villagers chosen by rotation. If a decision can't be reached, each party must provide a goat; both goats will have their legs cut open and filled with poison, and the owner of the goat which survives the longest is the winner. This system seems to date back to time immemorial, making Malana a credible contender for the world's oldest democracy.

I ask a few local people about who the Malana villagers are and where their culture originated, wondering if this caste-system fundamentalism perhaps represents an ossified form of the early Brahminic code somehow frozen on the passage between the Indus and the Ganges. Of course, they all tell me that they're the remnants of Alexander the Great's army.

The search for the identity of *soma* has turned out to be an odd, often impenetrable mixture of genuine scientific inquiry and something more like the search for the philosopher's stone — which, of course, *soma* in its later traditions comes so closely to resemble. This mixture is related to, but not reducible to, the shifting grey area in the Vedic tradition between Soma the god and *soma* the plant. On the one hand, the plant which is the source of *soma* is specifically referred to and described throughout both the Indian and Iranian traditions; on the other hand, any focused botanical analysis becomes dry and lifeless when divorced entirely from the broader spiritual world to which *soma* is the key. *Soma* inevitably comes to stand for the cosmic reality which underlies almost all religious traditions, but which has retained its original form in almost none. The Brahminic explanation that the plant itself was literally 'lost', or died out, seems to conceal a different story: that that particular realm of the gods became, in some way, permanently closed to humanity.

But, of all the possible plant candidates, *harmal* is certainly the most interesting tool with which to search for what *soma* must originally have been — just as drugs in general remain an incomparable tool to search for what *soma* originally represented. I've tried to follow the avenues which *harmal* opens up without becoming too attached to the *harmal/soma* theory: this is at times a rather tricky, zen-like balancing act, but is worth maintaining in order to avoid the habitual tendency in the history of *soma* studies to argue from one's conclusions.

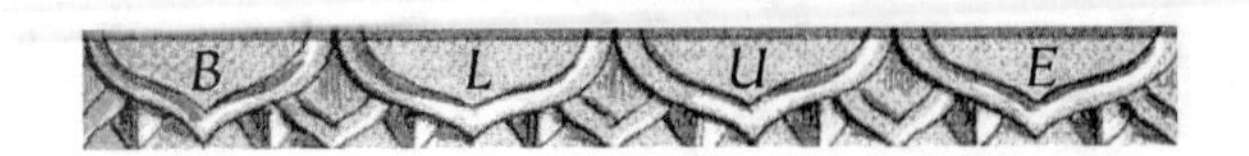

However, my visit to Ladakh has nudged me closer than I expected to a literal identification of *soma* and *harmal*. The evidence is that *harmal* use among the early Indo-European inhabitants of the Indus Valley must pre-date their current religious cultures; the inference is that *harmal*, at the very least, must have been part of the complex of sacred plants known to the Vedic *soma*-drinkers.

But I'm not satisfied that this is the end of the story. Even sifting through the levels of poetic eulogy, the *soma* described in the Vedas persistently sounds like a kind of roaring intoxication which is hard to square with the visionary trance which *harmal* produces. The *Arda Wiraz Namaq*, and other texts in the Iranian tradition with their cups of sleep and dream, sound far more like the now-familiar *harmal* experience.

There is an elegant solution to this discrepancy. Psilocybin mushrooms still grow in Nepal and the more easterly Himalayas, and are easily dried, preserved and transported. The combination of these mushrooms with *harmal* is effectively the Old World *ayahuasca*, a close chemical analogue with the same pineal interaction of tryptamines and beta-carbolines. Different admixtures of mushrooms and *harmal* can produce anything from a more physically intense variant of the *harmal* trip — as I discovered in Wales all those years ago — to the rushing intoxication I experienced in the Santo Daime ritual. It seems entirely plausible to locate all the various psychedelic states accorded to *soma* and *haoma* within the complexities of a mushroom/*harmal* brew, as well as the various references to drinkers of the "other *soma*/*haoma*" which Gershevitch has so delicately exposed. Its only drawback is the lack of a single shred of direct evidence to support it.

Once the idea of an Old World *ayahuasca* is mooted, the number of possible candidates can be, rather tentatively, extended. The Old World has fewer DMT-containing plants than the Americas, but certainly some which would have been accessible to the drinkers of *soma* and *haoma*. The giant river reed *Arundo Donax,* for example, is widespread across Central Asia and contains DMT, though in rather small quantities which are difficult to extract effectively and separate from the plant's toxins. Other sources of DMT exist, and still others may be waiting to be discovered. Gordon Hillman is currently working on a recent seed-find from a tomb at Abu Hureyra in Central Syria which dates from 8000BC and includes the charred seeds of *Zygophyllum Fabago,* a close *harmal* relative which suggests that the number of candidates may continue to grow.

☆ ☆

Recently, however, a new archaeological discovery has brought us closer than ever before to uncovering hard physical evidence of the existence and nature of the *soma* cult. In the Karakum desert of Turkmenistan, Russian archaeologists have unearthed the remains of a temple complex dating from around 1500BC which seems to have been used for the ritual preparation of a psychedelic drink, and to represent the culture of the 'Magi', the ancient Iranian tradition which Zoroaster inherited.

The temple seems to have had a fire-altar as its focus, and also a network of small "white rooms", with traces of white gypsum plaster still on their walls, set apart from the larger gathering-space and presumably the private domain of the priests. In one of these white rooms, ceramic vessels have been found: strainers with supports which would allow plant juice to flow through them and into a bowl placed below. The gypsum plaster in these rooms still contains microscopic traces of several plants, including ephedra, cannabis and opium pollen. On the floor by the ceramic strainers a bone tube or pipe has also been found, decorated with engraved images of exaggeratedly large eyes.

By the fire-altar, a sacred ash depository suggests that the fire of Agni burned while these potions were being

prepared and drunk. The altar itself has a bowl-shaped indentation with traces of greasy liquid still detectable. This room also contains a number of artefacts suggestive of the ceremony which would have taken place: a marble bull's head, amulets and engraved seals bearing images of men wearing animal masks and beating large tambourine-drums beneath the figure of Shamash, the Sumerian sun-god.

This site at Karakum gives us a more vivid picture than ever before of the cultic complex in which *soma* — or, more specifically, *haoma* — flourished. It's a picture which bears little relation to the image of classical antiquity which generations of Oriental scholars have painted. Unsurprisingly, perhaps, it seems far closer to many of the traditions which still survive around *ayahuasca* use in the Amazon: the ritual preparation of sacred brews brews prior to a ceremony where drumming and chanting bring the spirits of animals and gods down into the world of the worshippers.

It also enables us, at least by elimination, to be more specific about *soma* and *haoma's* botanical identity. First, it provides incontrovertible proof that a sophisticated tradition of psychedelic plant use did indeed exist among the early Indo-Iranians, and that its content can indeed be discovered. Second, it demonstrates that the sacred brew did, in some places at least, involve a complex of several plants. These two revelations destroy the vast majority of scholarly assertions about the identity of *soma*, and open up in their place a vast new field of study. Within this complex of knowledge, many plants — including, presumably, not only *harmal* but others we can only begin to guess at — would have had their place.

More than this, it offers a partial solution to the puzzle of why there are so many more traditions of psychedelic plant use in the New World than the Old. The Old World flora does indeed offer the potential for the complex ritual use of power plants, and this potential was, in the distant past, indeed realised.

Gone, but no longer forgotten.

☆ ☆

And, it appears, the rediscovery of this potential is already under way.

On the Santo Daime grapevine, I start to hear about a renegade offshoot of the Church which has set up in Amsterdam. Apparently it's run by a former priest who's 'given back her star', the term with the odd resonance of a rogue Western sheriff which means that she's resigned from the priesthood. I hear that the reason for this is that she wants to play down the heavily Christian framework of the rite and take it to its New Age Western clientele in a more rootsy, shamanic form.

This is confirmed when I'm given a copy of her flier: *"Friends of the Forest present: Quest For The Soul".* This offers a range of different *ayahuasca* rituals, clearly based on the Santo Daime working but tailored more specifically for different spiritual paths. The "Forest Journey" is the 'ethnic version' of the experience, featuring shamanic Amazon chants and channelled songs from Brazil. The "Heart Journey" is a quieter session, soft-pedalling the Amazon roots and accompanied instead by gentle New Age soundscapes. The "Trance Journey" is aimed at the post-rave crowd, using ambient house music to channel their chill-outs into more spiritual meditation.

Despite being exceptional in maintaining its use of the sacred psychedelic, the Santo Daime Church has, in the course of a single century, travelled the traditional route which took most of the older religions a thousand years or more. Its origins in the 1920s were in the exposure of a 'first stage' shamanic, tribal group mind to the outside world. Over the next generation, it evolved into a 'second stage' priestcraft, complete with a hierarchy organised around control of the supply of its central sacrament. Now, in Amsterdam, this in turn has transformed itself into a pluralistic 'third stage'

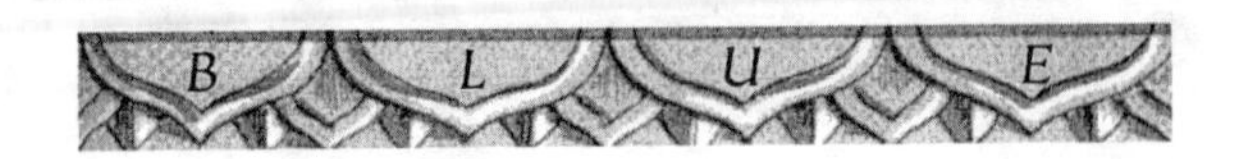

system which offers a range of alternative spiritual structures for the enlightenment-seeking individual.

I get into an email correspondence with Yatra, the woman behind the "Friends of the Forest" project, a Brazilian based in Amsterdam. She's very interested in *harmal*; in fact, she's been using it a great deal herself. Since giving back her star, it's been much more difficult for her to obtain the Church's *ayahuasca* brew, and she's been developing her own analogues, using *harmal* in place of the *yage* vine and a range of different DMT-containing forest shrubs.

I'm fascinated to discover that the process of rediscovery is moving in both directions. As well as taking her inspiration from Amazon shamanism, she's been taking her new-found knowledge back to them. She's introduced *harmal* to several tribes — the Atkum, the Caimbe, the Funio — who had lost the art of making an oral DMT brew, the lines of transmission having at some stage been broken. Having combined *harmal* with their DMT-containing mimosa, she tells me, they've now reverted enthusiastically to the long-forgotten practices of their ancestors — thanks to the long-forgotten practices of ours.

This is the kind of activity which demonstrates the ways in which the ancient 'group mind' of the *soma* model and the modern countercultural strategies of the Assassins are beginning to shade into each other, and maybe into something entirely new. At its roots in the Amazon, the *ayahuasca* rite remains perhaps the most striking survival of the primordial experience which *soma* represented. In the cities of Brazil, the Santo Daime Church still feeds and sustains the displaced fragments of a group mind fractured, often, only within living memory. In the form in which I experienced the Daime in London, it offered a glimpse of these origins, but one which was dispelled as soon as we stepped out again into the streets of Willesden as fellow-conspirators in an experience which would be impossible to explain to all but our closest friends. It may no longer be possible for most of us to surf the pure blue tide of the Vedic *soma*-drinkers, but it may still be that *harmal* and the other plants of power are capable of both less and more: giving us perhaps the faintest glimpse of the primordial realities of the past but, at the same time, taking us towards something new — something, perhaps, which we're still in the process of imagining.

BIBLIOGRAPHY

Abu-Rabia, Aref. *Negev Bedouin and Livestock Rearing* (Oxford, Berg, 1994).

Artaud, Antonin. *The Peyote Dance* (Farrar, Strauss & Giroux, 1976).

Bourke, John G. *Scatological Rites of All Nations* (1891).

Boyce, Mary. *Zoroastrianism: Its Age and Constant Vigour* (Mazda Publishers, 1992).

Burroughs, William. *The Yage Letters* (City Lights Books, 1963); *Naked Lunch* (Olympia Press, 1959).

Callaway, J. C. "Tryptamines, Beta-Carbolines and You," (*MAPS Journal* Vol. 4, #2).

Chohan, Amar Singh. *A Historical Study of Society and Culture in Dardistan and Ladakh* (Altantic Publishers, New Delhi, 1983).

Clark, Graham E. "Who Were The Dards?" (*Kailash,* Vol. 5/4, 1977).

Cohn, Norman. *Cosmos, Chaos and the World to Come* (Yale University Press, 1993).

Daftary, Farhad. *The Assassin Legends: Myths of the Isma'ilis* (I. B.Tauris, 1995).

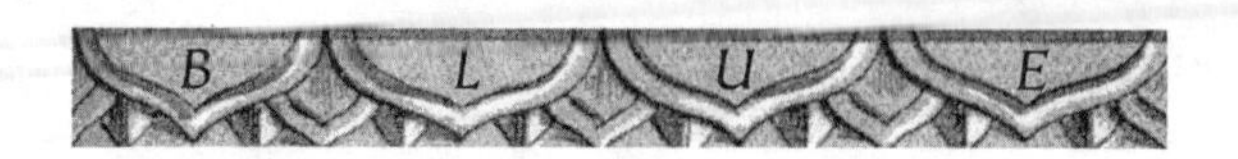

Devereux, Paul. *The Long Trip* (Penguin Arkana, 1997).
Doniger, Wendy, (ed). *The Rig Veda* (Penguin, 1981);
——— *The Laws of Manu* (Penguin, 1991).
Durkheim, Émile. *The Elementary Forms of Religious Life* (Allen & Unwin, 1915).
Emboden, William. *Narcotic Plants* (Studio Vista, London, 1972).
Flattery, David Stophet and Schwartz, Martin. *Haoma And Harmaline* (University of California Near Eastern Studies Vol. 21, 1989).
Francke, A. H. *A History of Western Tibet* (S. W. Partridge, 1907).
Frawley, David. *Gods, Sages and Kings* (Passage Press, Utah, 1991).
Fuller, John. *The Day of St. Anthony's Fire* (Macmillan, US, 1968).
Furst, Peter T. (ed.) *Flesh of the Gods: The Ritual Uses of Hallucinogens* (Waveland Press, Illinois, US, 1990).
Gaultier, Theophile. *Club des Hashishins* (1872).
Gershevitch, Ilya. *An Iranist's View of the Soma Controversy* (Fondation Culturelle Iranienne, 1974).
Gorman, Peter. *Divine Smoke and God's Flesh* (Best of *High Times,* Vol. 17).
Hassan, Ikram. "Some Folk Uses of Peganum Harmala in India and Pakistan" (*Journal of Economic Botany* Vol. 21, 1967).
Hillebrandt, Alfred. *Vedic Mythology* (Breslau, 1891–1902).
Hinnells, John R., (ed). *Dictionary of Religions* (Penguin, 1984).
Jettmar, Karl. *The Religions of the Hindu-Kush* (Oxford & IBH Publishing, 1986).
Kamen-Kaye, Dorothy. "What Was Palgrave's Plant?" (*Revista de la Academia Columbiana* #63, 1988).
Kaul, M. K. *Medicinal Plants of Kashmir and Ladakh* (Indus Publishing, New Delhi, 1997).
Lamb, Bruce F. *Wizard of the Upper Amazon* (North Atlantic Books, 1971).
Lewin, Lewis. *Phantastica: Narcotic and Stimulating Drugs, Their Use and Abuse* (1931).
Lilly, John. *The Centre of the Cyclone* (Paladin, 1977).
Linnaeus. *Inebrianta* (Upsaliae, 1762).

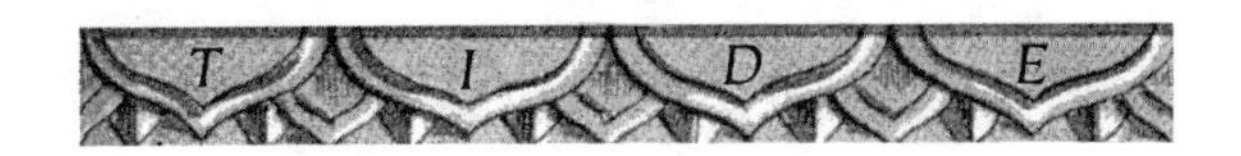

Mallory, J. P. *In Search of the Indo-Europeans* (Thames & Hudson, 1979).

Mills, L. H., (tr.). *Hom Yasht* (Sacred Books of the East, 1898).

Mooney, James. *The Ghost-Dance Religion and the Sioux Outbreak of 1890* (Bureau of American Ethnology, 1986).

Moreau de Tours, J. J. *Hashish and Mental Illness* (Raven Press, 1972).

Naranjo, Claudio. *The Healing Journey: New Approaches to Consciousness* (Hutchinson, 1973).

Navchoo, Irshad and Buth, G.M. "Ethnobotany of Ladakh, India: Beverages, Narcotics, Food" (*Journal of Economic Botany* 44 (3), 1990).

Oldenberg, Hermann. *The Religion of the Vedas* (Motilal Banarsidass, Delhi, 1988).

Ott, Jonathan. *Pharmacotheon* (1993).

Ramanathan, A. S. *The Vedic Concept of Soma* (Rajastan Patrika, Jaipur 1995).

Peissel, Michel. *The Ants' Gold: The Discovery of the Greek El Dorado in the Himalayas* (Harvill Press, 1984).

Ratsch, Christian. *Dictionary of Sacred and Magical Plants* (Prism Press, 1992).

Reichel-Dolmatoff, G. "Drug-Induced Optical Sensations and their Relationship to Applied Art among some Colombian Indians" (in *Art and Society,* ed. Michael Greenhalgh and Vincent Megaw, Duckworth, 1978).

Rudgley, Richard. *The Alchemy of Culture: Intoxicants in Society* (British Museum Press 1993).

——— *Encyclopaedia of Psychoactive Substances* (Little, Brown, UK, 1998).

Sadoul, Jacques. *Alchemists and Gold* (Neville Spearman, 1971).

Sandars, N. K., (tr.). *Epic of Gilgamesh* (Penguin, 1960).

Sarianidi, Viktor. "Temples of Bronze Age Margiana: traditions of ritual architecture" (*Antiquity* 68 [1994]: 388–97).

Schleiffer, Hedwig. *Narcotic Plants of the Old World* (Lubrecht & Crauer, 1979).

Shulgin, Alexander. *Tikhal* (Transform Press, US 1997).

Schultes, Richard Evans and Hoffman, Albert. *Plants of the Gods* (Healing Arts Press, 1992).

Schwartz, Martin. *Cambridge History of Iran* (Cambridge University Press, 1985).

Stafford, Peter. *Psychedelics Encyclopaedia* (Ronin Publishing, 1992).

Staten Island Project. *The Ibogaine Story* (Autonomedia, 1997).

Stewart, Omer C. *Peyote Religion: A History* (University of Oklahoma Press, 1987).

Strassman, R. J. "The Pineal Gland: Current Evidence for its Role in Consciousness" (*Psychedelic Monographs and Essays,* Vol. 5, 1991).

Vahman, Fereydun, (ed). *Arda Wiraz Namaq: The Iranian 'Divina Commedia'* (Curzon Press, 1986).

Wasson, Gordon R. "Seeking the Magic Mushroom" (*Life Magazine,* May 13, 1957).

——— *Soma: Divine Mushroom of Immortality* (Harcourt Brace Jovanovich, 1968).

Wasson, Gordon R., Hoffman, Albert, and Ruck, Carl A. P. *The Road to Eleusis* (Harcourt Brace Jovanovich, 1978).

Zaehner, R. C. *The Dawn and Twilight of Zoroastrianism* (Wiedenfeld & Nicholson, London, 1961).

Zoja, Luigi. *Drugs, Addiction and Initiation: The Modern Search for Ritual* (Sigo Press, Boston, 1989).

Also From Autonomedia Publishers And Distributors

DREAMER OF THE DAY Francis Parker Yockey and the Postwar Fascist Underground Kevin Coogan
PSYCHEDELICS REIMAGINED Tom Lyttle, ed. Foreword by Hakim Bey, Introduction by Timothy Leary
BLUE TIDE The Search for Soma Mike Jay
T.A.Z. The Temporary Autonomous Zone, Ontological Anarchy, Poetic Terrorism Hakim Bey
AVANT GARDENING Ecological Struggles in the City & the World Peter Lamborn Wilson and Bill Weinberg, eds.
CASSETTE MYTHOS The New Music Underground Robin James, ed.
FRIENDLY FIRE Bob Black
CRIMES OF CULTURE Richard Kostelanetz
POLITICAL ESSAYS Richard Kostelanetz
MAGPIE REVERIES The Iconographic Mandalas of James Koehnline
ESCAPE FROM THE 19TH CENTURY Essays on Fourier, Marx, Nietzsche & Proudhon Peter Lamborn Wilson
INVISIBLE GOVERNANCE The Art of African Micropolitics D. Hecht & Maliqalim Simone
ON ANARCHY & SCHIZOANALYSIS Rolando Perez
GOD & PLASTIC SURGERY Marx, Nietzsche, Freud & the Obvious Jeremy Barris
MARX BEYOND MARX Lessons on the Grundrisse Antonio Negri
MODEL CHILDREN Inside the Republic of Red Scarves Paul Thorez
ABOUT FACE Race in Postmodern America Maliqalim Simone
COLUMBUS & OTHER CANNIBALS The Wétiko Disease & the White Man Jack Forbes
METATRON Sol Yurick
SCANDAL Essays in Islamic Heresy Peter Lamborn Wilson
HORSEXE Essay on Transsexuality Catherine Millot
THE TOUCH Michael Brownstein
ARCANE OF REPRODUCTION Housework, Prostitution, Labor & Capital Leopoldina Fortunati
TROTSKYISM & MAOISM A. Belden Fields
FILM & POLITICS IN THE THIRD WORLD John Downing, ed.
ENRAGÉS & SITUATIONISTS IN THE OCCUPATION MOVEMENT René Viénet
MIDNIGHT OIL Work, Energy, War, 1973 – 1992 Midnight Notes
PURE WAR Paul Virilio & Sylvère Lotringer
WALKING THROUGH CLEAR WATER IN A POOL PAINTED BLACK Cookie Mueller
STILL BLACK, STILL STRONG Dhoruba bin Wahad, Mumia Abu-Jamal, Assata Shakur
HANNIBAL LECTER, MY FATHER Kathy Acker
METATRON Sol Yurick
HOW I BECAME ONE OF THE INVISIBLE David Rattray
GONE TO CROATAN Origins of North American Dropout Culture Sakolsky & Koehnline, eds.
SEMIOTEXT(E) ARCHITECTURE Hraztan Zeitlian, ed.
SEMIOTEXT(E) USA Jim Fleming & Peter Lamborn Wilson, eds.
OASIS Maliqalim Simone, et al., eds.
POLYSEXUALITY François Peraldi, ed.
THE ARCHEOLOGY OF VIOLENCE Pierre Clastres
FATAL STRATEGIES Jean Baudrillard
THE LOST DIMENSION Paul Virilio
THE AESTHETICS OF DISAPPEARANCE Paul Virilio
NOT ME Eileen Myles
SICK BURN CUT Deran Ludd
69 WAYS TO PLAY THE BLUES Jürg Laederach
POPULAR DEFENSE & ECOLOGICAL STRUGGLES Paul Virilio
CRACKING THE MOVEMENT Squatting Beyond the Media Foundation for the Advancement of Illegal Knowledge
SEMIOTEXT(E) SF Rudy Rucker, Robert Anton Wilson & Peter Lamborn Wilson, eds.
BOLO'BOLO P.M.
SIMULATIONS Jean Baudrillard
GERMANIA Heiner Müller
COMMUNISTS LIKE US Félix Guattari & Toni Negri
THE ECSTASY OF COMMUNICATION Jean Baudrillard
IN THE SHADOW OF THE SILENT MAJORITIES Jean Baudrillard
FORGET FOUCAULT Jean Baudrillard
FOUCAULT LIVE Michel Foucault
LOOKING BACK ON THE END OF THE WORLD Baudrillard, Virilio, et al.
REMARKS ON MARX Michel Foucault
IF YOU'RE A GIRL Ann Rower
SPEED AND POLITICS Paul Virilio
NOMADOLOGY: THE WAR MACHINE Gilles Deleuze & Félix Guattari
ON THE LINE Gilles Deleuze & Félix Guattari
DRIFTWORKS Jean-François Lyotard
THE MADAME REALISM COMPLEX Lynne Tillman
THE DAMNED UNIVERSE OF CHARLES FORT Louis Kaplan
RADIOTEXT(E) Neil Strauss, Dave Mandl, eds.